Commission to review allowances of
Members of Parliament

SUPPORTING
DEMOCRACY

Volume 2
Research Papers

© 1998 Minister of Public Works and Government Services
ISBN 0-662-63315-6
Catalogue No. CP 32-61/1997

CONTENTS

INTRODUCTION

This volume contains seven research papers prepared to assist the Commission to Review Allowances of Members of Parliament in its deliberations.

The first six papers were prepared by the Commission's staff to provide background on several areas related to remuneration and benefits for Canada's Members of Parliament:*

- work done by previous commissions to review members' allowances
- the current situation with regard to members' pay and benefits
- historical background on how members' compensation has evolved and what its relative value is today
- comparisons with the compensation packages offered legislators elsewhere in Canada and the world and with the remuneration of senior federal public servants in Canada
- the content and value of the work done by Members of the House of Commons
- the effects of service in the House of Commons on subsequent financial situation and career prospects

The seventh report, reviewing pension and benefits arrangements for members of the Senate and the House of Commons, was prepared for the Commission by William M. Mercer Limited of Ottawa.

As commissioned papers, these reports remain the work of the authors and do not necessarily reflect the individual or collective views of commissioners on the subjects covered.

---

* In this volume, as elsewhere in the Commission's report, we use 'Members of Parliament' as the collective term for members of the Senate and members of the House of Commons.

**Previous Commissions to Review
Allowances of Members of Parliament:
Recommendations and Results**

RESEARCH
PAPER 1

CONTENTS

Research Paper 1

Previous Commissions to Review Allowances of Members of Parliament: Recommendations and Results

The purpose of this paper is to review the contents of reports by previous commissions to review allowances of Members of Parliament, with a view to building on earlier results and avoiding duplication. The goal is to examine the main arguments made by other commissions and to determine the extent to which their recommendations were implemented.

A provision concerning a statutory commission to review compensation for parliamentarians was added to the *Parliament of Canada Act* following the 1970 recommendations of the Beaupré committee, an advisory committee appointed to review parlimentary salaries and expenses. After each election, a commission is appointed and must report within a six-month statutory deadline. The next section is organized in reverse chronological order, beginning with the most recent commission. For each report, the following information is provided:

- summaries of the contents, including main themes or issues examined, research and analysis conducted, and recommendations made
- the results of the commission's work (the extent to which recommendations were implemented)

Contents of Previous Reports

There have been five previous commissions to review the allowances of Members of Parliament. The commissions (which are generally referred to by the name of the chairperson or members), along with the dates of their reports, are as follows:

- the Lapointe commission, 1994
- the St. Germain-Fox commission, 1989
- the Clarke-Campbell commission, 1985
- the McIsaac-Balcer commission, 1980
- the Hales commission, 1979

The Lapointe Commission

The Lapointe commission, chaired by the Honourable Charles Lapointe, with Jean Piggott and C.E.S. Franks as members, was appointed after the 1993 election and reported in 1994. The commission's stated goal was to reinvigorate democratic institutions and restore the public's faith in political institutions and in politicians.

The commission's analysis of the situation regarding compensation for parliamentarians was premised on several observations: that Canadians do not understand what democratic representation is all about; that parliamentarians themselves fail to explain the democratic process to their constituents; and that the news media report only part of the story. Commissioners also saw confusion about what Members of Parliament are actually paid for and whether their remuneration is fair, given the functions they perform. In addition, there is no mechanism to ensure that members are accountable for their incidental expense allowance. Finally, commissioners observed that the goals and details of the retirement plan are not clear.

The Lapointe commission therefore set out to understand what the job of a parliamentarian is; to determine what level of remuneration is fair for the work done; to establish clear goals for members' compensation package, including the retirement plan; and to ensure that members are accountable for the way they spend the expense allowance.

To complete these tasks, the commission adopted a four-part methodology:
- They defined what members do by using readily identifiable functions, then calculated the amount of time spent by members at each function.
- They asked members about the adequacy of compensation.
- They compared functions with comparable jobs in the private and public sectors.
- They compared Canadian parliamentarians' compensation with that of legislators in other countries.

A central theme in the Lapointe commission's discussion of compensation for parliamentarians was the lack of knowledge on which to base public debate. While recognizing that there are inadequacies in the current pay scale, the commission noted that politicians and political institutions are generally held in low public esteem. Moreover, most Canadians lack a clear idea of what MPs actually do, and they are no better informed about the basis on which politicians are paid. This level of public dissatisfaction, combined with the low level of knowledge, does not allow for informed, dispassionate debate on the issue of compensation. Yet if major changes in the compensation package are contemplated, such a discussion is required.

Recommendations

The commission's recommendations regarding the sessional indemnity — that it be raised to $75,000, with a second increase to $86,000 after the next election — were not implemented. Nor was the commission's proposal to replace the incidental expense allowance and the travel status allowance with an accountable accommodation allowance (that is, receipts needed) of $15,000 and a work-related expense allowance of $10,000 ($6,000 for members of the Senate).

Two of the Lapointe commission's recommendations were adopted:
- The practice of double dipping (that is, receiving both a parliamentary pension and remuneration from a subsequent federal appointment, employment or service contract accepted after 13 July 1995) was eliminated by Bill C-85 in 1995. Pensions are now reduced by the amount by which such remuneration exceeds $5,000 in any 12-month period.
- The age of eligibility for a parliamentary pension was raised to 55 (instead of the date on which the member resigned or was defeated).

The St. Germain-Fox Commission

The 1989 recommendations of the St. Germain-Fox commission (appointed after the 1988 election and consisting of the Honourable Gerry St. Germain and the Honourable Francis Fox) focused on ensuring that the most capable people were attracted to and retained in public life. The commission believed that this would promote a more representative and effective system of government. It gathered information through a questionnaire sent to members and former members of the House of Commons and conducted or commissioned research on legislators' remuneration in Canada and abroad.

In commissioners' view, the issues involved were essentially twofold: First, do Canadians want the most qualified people governing the country? Second, are we prepared to compensate them adequately to ensure this?

Recommendations

The commission's main recommendations were as follows (with the results provided in parentheses):

- Increase the sessional indemnity by 4 per cent after the next election. (Not implemented; instead, the indemnity was increased by 0.35 per cent.)
- Tighten penalties for non-attendance in the Senate. (Not implemented.)
- Increase the allowance for MPs with extra responsibilities, such as committee chairpersons. (Not implemented.)
- Establish an accountable accommodation allowance of $6,000 for MPs. (Introduced in October 1990.)
- Base indexing of indemnity and allowances on the average of the Consumer Price Index and the Industrial Aggregate Index. (*Parliament of Canada Act* amended in 1993 to take both indexes into account.)
- Extend severance allowance for defeated MPs to those not entitled to a pension and who are still unemployed six months to a year after their defeat. (Allowance established at 50 per cent of basic annual sessional indemnity and of any additional indemnity paid to an MP for additional responsibilities.)
- To improve the appearance of impartiality in the process to review members' allowances, future commissions should include non-parliamentarians, and their recommendations should apply only after the next election. (Not implemented.)

The Clarke-Campbell Commission

The members of this commission, which was appointed after the 1984 election and reported the next year, were William H. Clarke and Coline Campbell, both former members of the House of Commons. The commission sought public input through newspaper advertisements and sent questionnaires to members of the House of Commons and the Senate, as well as MPs in the previous parliament who did not return.

Commissioners saw a need to adhere to several principles in remunerating parliamentarians:

- openness with the public to ensure that the basis for parliamentary salaries was well understood by Canadians;
- fairness of members' remuneration compared with what other Canadians were earning and the way that changed over time; and
- discretion and flexibility for members in the way the compensation package was structured and administered.

The commission concluded that it was preferable to link the salary of the legislator to the economy as a whole, thereby reflecting the earning capacity of Canadians at large at any particular period of time. Such a basis for remuneration is easily comprehensible to the ordinary Canadian.

In addition, commissioners stated in their report, parliamentary salaries should be based on

the average earnings of Canadians rather than on a measure of inflation. In this way any future increase or decrease in the salary we pay to legislators will reflect what people earn rather than what they can buy with their dollar... Given the executive nature of the job, and the heavy workload and irregular schedule involved, the Commission also concluded that MPs' salaries should be three times the Average Annual Earnings. (Report, pp. 25-26)

Commissioners also asserted that parliamentarians should not "be forced to bear the expense of holding office personally" and rejected the idea of tying members' remuneration to that of executives in the public service, believing that this could create the appearance of a conflict of interest in negotiations to establish public servants' salaries.

Recommendations

The Clarke-Campbell commission recommended setting the annual remuneration of MPs at $69,000, calling it a salary, and adjusting it each year by the percentage change in the annual average of the industrial aggregate for the previous year. The incidental expense allowance should be abolished, the commission said, to be replaced by a daily living and accommodation allowance of $100 for each sitting day of the Commons or a committee or $25 while in the constituency.

The MP's office budget was also to be restructured, with one global amount to be provided in place of the office budget, the constituency spending allowance, the constituency travel allowance, and the equipment allowance.

A severance allowance was recommended for MPs not re-elected, consisting of one month's pay for each year of service, to a maximum of 24 years, to be paid in monthly amounts. The allowance would not be available, however, to former members who were entitled to a parliamentary pension or accepted a position in the federal sector.

Just two of the Clarke-Campbell commission's recommendations were implemented: an improvement in the pension available to members of the Senate, and a supplement to the global budget for MPs with larger constituencies.

The McIsaac-Balcer Commission

Reporting in 1980, after the election of the same year, the McIsaac-Balcer commission (Dr. Cliff McIsaac and the Honourable Léon Balcer) based its conclusions and recommendations on a review of previous reports on the subject from Canada, the United States, Australia and the United Kingdom; an examination of the remuneration paid to provincial legislators and members of city councils in large urban areas; discussions with members of the House of Commons and the Senate; and consultations with the private sector, including organized labour. The commission also sought public input through newspaper advertisements.

Recurring themes in the commission's report included fairness and equity, flexibility, and accountability. As commissioners saw the issues:

> Two fundamental questions [must] be faced head-on — do we as citizens want to have the most capable people in Parliament governing the country, and if so, are we prepared to compensate them adequately so they can do the best possible job....
>
> If Canadians want their parliamentarians to do a better job, then they must be prepared to pay. Similarly, if Members of Parliament are serious about doing the best job possible, they should have the courage to give themselves the proper tools to do just that. (p. 3)

The commission stated that the issue of remuneration should be approached in a sound, rational manner and that any increases should rely on a rationale based on the general occupational characteristics of the job of being a member of the House of Commons or the Senate. At the same time, the commission believed that

> present Members are entitled to such an increase, and Canadians should not expect MPs to lose financially or suffer disrupted and broken careers in order to serve in public office. We are further convinced that only by making salary levels attractive will Canadians be ensured that the highest calibre of people from all walks of life will feel free to seek this important elected office. (pp. 7-8)

Commissioners were concerned that the remuneration of federal legislators seemed to have lost ground relative to that of provincial and municipal elected officials and that this and other aspects of political life were taking their toll on recruitment:

> Officials of major political parties in Canada told us in discussions that the pay levels coupled with the 'public abuse factor' were cited frequently by potential candidates as reasons for not seeking nomination. (p. 7)

Recommendations

The McIsaac-Balcer commission recommended increasing the remuneration of MPs and senators in line with that of professional and managerial employees in the private and public sectors, phasing the increase in over a four-year period. At the same time, the commission said, the incidental expense allowance should be reduced and tied to the Consumer Price Index. In addition, an accommodation allowance should be introduced, because the commission's research had shown that almost half the MPs' incidental expense allowance was being spent on accommodation.

Travel costs should be completely reimbursed for travel within an MP's constituency, upon presentation of receipts, and all travel expenditures should be fully disclosed on a quarterly basis.

Finally, a severance allowance should be introduced for MPs who did not qualify for a pension.

After the commission's report, the sessional indemnity for MPs was increased over four years and that of senators in two phases, and by more than the recommended amount. A severance allowance was established for defeated MPs, and services and office space were improved. Although the commission recommended that the non-accountable expense allowance for MPs be reduced and that for senators remain unchanged, it was increased in both cases.

The Hales Commission

The report of commissioner Alfred D. Hales, following the election of 1979, was based on interviews with MPs and senators and a review of the U.S. system for compensating members of Congress. Mr. Hales surveyed members using a questionnaire covering such issues as remuneration, housing, transportation, services, constituency operating costs, financial needs, and other aspects of the compensation package. Two-thirds of the members responded.

In his report, Mr. Hales stated that MPs were "grossly underpaid", given that the workload had increased significantly over the previous five years and their work week was now 70 to 80 hours. Commissioner Hales' concern was that a time would come when only those who could afford it would run for public office.

Members should not have to vote for their own increase, but nor should increases be automatic. MPs' remuneration should be comparable to that in other occupations, given the long work week and the need to provide services in the ridings. The salary should be completely divorced from expense allowances, however, to permit comparisons with other occupations.

Commissioner Hales thought that the budget system should be flexible, to reflect the varying cost of meeting constituency needs in diverse ridings. Thus, a global budget, "directly related to the actual cost of serving a riding", should replace the incidental expense allowance, allowing surpluses in one expenditure area to be transferred to other areas of greater need. Members sought flexibility, equality, fairness and a sense of pride in managing their own affairs, the commissioner wrote, but there was also a need for "an incentive to practise economy".

Recommendations

Mr. Hales' recommendation for an increase in the sessional indemnity was accepted, but the recommendation to replace the incidental expense allowance with a series of specialized allowances was not implemented. Nor was the suggestion that the various indemnities and allowances, including the extra amounts paid to those with additional responsibilities, be reviewed by an advisory board established for the purpose.

The recommendation that specific budgets be established for expenses such as operating a constituency office, staffing, stationery and printing, and telephone services was accepted, however, as was the recommendation for a travel allowance based on the cost of 52 return trips by air between Ottawa and the location of the member's residence or constituency office.

Summary and Comparisons

In this section we examine some of the common themes or issues apparent in the reports of the five commissions to date and compare their respective approaches in three areas of compensation: the sessional indemnity, the incidental expense allowance, and other remuneration and allowances.

Common Themes

In discussions of the remuneration of Members of Parliament, some issues or themes have resurfaced repeatedly in the reports of these commissions. For example,

- Parliament is valuable as an institution and should be maintained as an institution that functions effectively and smoothly. To do this requires the election and retention of competent, qualified people, and good pay is required to attract good people.
- The work that MPs do is roughly comparable to that done by middle-upper level professionals. MPs work long hours and have many demands and pressures on them that most people do not face, and they should not be expected to cover all the expenses occasioned by their life as MPs from their own pockets.
- MPs should not become wealthy or profit excessively as a result of their public service, nor should MPs see their pay increase when other Canadians are suffering financial hardship.
- MPs vote for their own increases, and this constitutes a conflict of interest.
- Regardless of any determination of what constitutes fair compensation for the value of the work they do, MPs' remuneration must be consistent with public expectations, and public expectations may in fact require that MPs be paid less than a fair amount.

Sessional Indemnities

Every commission has recommended that the sessional indemnity be increased, but they differed in how the increase should be made.

The first commission (Hales, 1979) recommended increasing MPs' sessional indemnity by a lump sum, with no change for members of the Senate.

The McIsaac-Balcer commission of 1980 recommended a four-phase increase to bring MPs' remuneration into line with that of their professional and managerial peers in the public and private sectors, with a two-phase increase for senators.

In 1985 the Clarke-Campbell commission recommended a lump-sum increase, to be reviewed every year and amended to reflect changes in the Industrial Aggregate Index. Senators' pay was to be fixed at 60 per cent of MPs' basic sessional indemnity.

The St. Germain-Fox commission of 1989 recommended a 4-per cent increase in the sessional indemnity.

The Lapointe commission (1994) recommended that the remuneration of members of the House of Commons and the Senate be increased after the freeze on public-sector wages was lifted, with a further increase only after the next election.

Incidental Expense Allowance

The incidental expense allowance was treated differently by each commission, with no consensus on the amount, its status, or how it should be changed.

The Hales commission recommended replacing the incidental expense allowance with specialized allowances that "should be used only to offset expenses incurred. ...under no circumstances should it be used to bolster a Member's basic pay".

The McIsaac-Balcer commission recommended reducing the incidental expense allowance to $7,000 and linking it to the Consumer Price Index. Senators' expense allowance was to remain at $6,000.

The Clarke-Campbell commission recommended eliminating the allowance, which, it said, "has been viewed as a supplemental salary for MPs".

The St. Germain-Fox commission recommended that the incidental expense allowance be changed only after the next election and that all future changes be linked to a formula based on changes in the Consumer Price Index and the Industrial Aggregate Index.

Finally, the Lapointe commission recommended replacing the incidental expense allowance with a $15,000 accommodation allowance, a $10,000 work-related expense allowance, and an extra provision for those representing larger ridings.

Other Allowances and Services

Neither the amount nor the method of determining the amount of other allowances or indemnities was consistent in the recommendations of previous commissions.

The Hales commission saw all other expense allowances being included in a global budget, with flexibility for MPs to allocate funds for various purposes within that budget and changes in rates being based on the recommendations of an advisory board or committee.

The McIsaac-Balcer commission recommended that travel costs within an MP's constituency be paid in full on submission of receipts and that the amount paid for expenses be disclosed regularly.

The Clarke-Campbell commission recommended an additional indemnity for committee chairpersons and others with extra responsibilities, along with a per diem expense and accommodation allowance in place of the incidental expense allowance.

The St. Germain-Fox commission recommended an accountable accommodation allowance limited to $6,000 for MPs only, with changes in this and other allowances linked to changes in the Consumer Price Index and the Industrial Aggregate Index.

The Lapointe commission recommended improving public accountability for the use of expense allowances by publishing a detailed annual summary of MPs' expenses. The commission also recommended the end of double-dipping.

Implemented Recommendations

The recommendations made by the commissions and implemented by Parliament help to trace how members' compensation has evolved over the past two decades.

The Hales commission suggested that the sessional indemnity be increased, and it was, by a much greater amount than what was recommended. The salary schedule for members with additional responsibilities was also revised. Specific budgets were set for several categories of expenses — constituency office operations, staffing, stationery and printing, and telephone services — and a committee was established to determine the rate of adjustment for these budgets. MPs and Senators received a transportation allowance based on the cost of 52 return trips by air between Ottawa and the member's residence or constituency office.

After the McIsaac-Balcer commission reported in 1980, the sessional indemnity for MPs was increased over four years and that of senators in two phases, and by more than the recommended amount. A severance allowance was established for defeated MPs, and services and office space were improved. Although the commission recommended that the non-accountable expense allowance for MPs be reduced and that for senators remain unchanged, it was increased in both cases.

The many recommendations of the Clarke-Campbell commission in 1985 resulted in just two changes: an improvement in pension arrangements for members of the Senate, and a supplement to the global budget for large constituencies.

Sessional indemnities for members of both the Senate and the House of Commons were increased after the report of the St. Germain-Fox commission, but by a smaller amount than recommended (0.35 per cent instead of 4 per cent). Future increases were indexed to an average of the Consumer Price Index and the Industrial Aggregate Index. The severance allowance for defeated MPs was set at 50 per cent of the annual sessional indemnity plus any allowance provided for extra responsibilities. The accountable accommodation allowance for MPs was limited to $6,000 a year.

On the recommendation of the Lapointe commission, the age of eligibility for a parliamentary pension was raised to 55, with provision for earlier payout in special cases (such as disability). Also as a result of this commission's work, the practice of double-dipping was ended.

Appendix
Previous Reports and Research

1994

Commission to Review Allowances of Members of Parliament (the Lapointe Commission), *Democratic Ideals and Financial Realities, Paying Representatives in the 21st Century* (Ottawa: Minister of Supply and Services, 1994).

Research studies

Robert Burge, "Canadian Perceptions of Politics, Politicians and the Remuneration of Members of Parliament", April 1994.

J.A.W. Gunn, "Remuneration of the Canadian MP — The Arguments Considered", April 1994.

Louis Massicotte, "La rémunération des parlementaires fédéraux", April 1994.

Angus Reid Group, "Survey to examine public attitudes toward the salaries of Members of Parliament", March 1994.

1989

Commission to Review Allowances of Members of Parliament (the St. Germain-Fox commission), (Ottawa: 1989).

1985

Report of the Commission to Review Salaries of Members of Parliament and Senators (the Clarke-Campbell commission), (Ottawa: 1985).

1980

Report of the Commission to Review Salaries of Members of Parliament and Senators (the McIsaac-Balcer commission), (Ottawa: 1980).

1979

Report of the Commission to Review Salaries and Allowances of Members of Parliament and Senators (the Hales commission), (Ottawa: 1979).

Other Studies

There have been three other Canadian studies of remuneration for federal parliamentarians:

Report of the Advisory Committee on Parliamentary Salaries and Expenses (the Beaupré report), 1970.
Report of the Advisory Commission on Parliamentary Accommodation (the Abbott report), 1976.
Sobeco Ernst & Young, *Parliamentarians' Compensation,* a study commissioned by the Treasury Board, 1994.

The Allowances and Benefits of
Members of Parliament:
Current Amounts and a Brief History

RESEARCH
PAPER 2

CONTENTS

Research Paper 2

The Allowances and Benefits of Members of Parliament: Current Amounts and a Brief History

The remuneration of Members of Parliament takes two main forms: a sessional indemnity (referred to in the law as the sessional allowance and known more commonly as the salary) and an incidental expense allowance (sometimes included in statements of members' salary but not in fact part of it). This paper provides an overview of the remuneration and allowances of Members of Parliament (that is, members of both the Senate and the House of Commons), along with the various other benefits and services provided to them. We begin with members of the House of Commons.

Remuneration and Benefits for Members of the House of Commons

The sessional indemnity and incidental expense allowance for members of the House of Commons are established by the *Parliament of Canada Act,* which also provides for annual adjustments. Since passage of *Government Expenditures Restraint Act, 1993,* however, these amounts have been frozen. After public service remuneration was frozen under the *Public Sector Compensation Act,* members' sessional indemnity and incidental expense allowance were frozen at 1991 levels ($64,400 and $21,300-$28,200 respectively) for 1992, 1993, 1994 and 1995. In June 1994, the freeze was extended to December 31, 1997.

Sessional Indemnity

Eligibility for payment commences on the date of a member's election, and the indemnity is paid monthly. These payments continue until the date a successor is elected (following dissolution) unless, at an earlier date, the seat is vacated by resignation or for another reason. In the event of death, the sessional allowance is paid to the end of the month in which death occurs, and the expense allowance is paid up to and including the day of death.

In the absence of the freeze, the sessional indemnity would be adjusted annually, on January 1, in accordance with the *Parliament of Canada Act.* The adjustment would be calculated as the lesser of the change in the Industrial Aggregate minus one per cent or the change in the Consumer Price Index minus one per cent.[1]

---

1   The Industrial Aggregate measures the increase in the average weekly salaries and wages of Canadians. The Consumer Price Index measures changes in the cost of a basket of consumer goods.

Members receive additional remuneration for extra duties performed as prime minister; cabinet minister; secretary of state; speaker or deputy speaker; deputy chairperson or assistant deputy chairperson of the committee of the whole (assistant speakers); leader, house leader, whip or deputy whip of recognized parties; or parliamentary secretary.

Incidental Expense Allowance

Members' incidental expense allowance is paid and, in the absence of the current freeze, would be adjusted annually under the *Parliament of Canada Act* on the same basis as the sessional indemnity.

Most members receive an incidental expense allowance of $21,300. Members representing electoral districts that are remote or difficult to reach (24 members at present) receive $26,200 per year, paid annually. The two members for the Northwest Territories are entitled to $28,200 per year. The incidental expense allowance is not subject to income tax, nor is it necessary to provide receipts to document expenses.

Retirement Benefits

The *Members of Parliament Retiring Allowances Act* was introduced in 1952 to provide pension coverage for members of the House of Commons and was amended most recently in 1995. The act stipulates the following in respect of members of the House of Commons:

- Members' contributions are equal to 9 per cent of the sessional indemnity. These contributions are used to purchase further pensionable service credits and increase the retiring allowance payable.
- Members receiving an additional indemnity as prime minister, cabinet minister, secretary of state, speaker, deputy speaker, deputy chair or assistant deputy chair, party leader, house leader, whip, deputy whip, or parliamentary secretary have the option of contributing up to 9 per cent of these additional amounts as well.
- A minimum of six years of service in the House of Commons is needed to qualify for a pension. Pensions are paid at the rate of 4 per cent per year of service based on the average of the six best consecutive years of earnings. Pensions are limited to a maximum of 75 per cent of pre-retirement earnings (after 19 years of service).
- A pension is payable to a former member at age 55, or earlier if the former member is disabled. In the event of the death of a member or former member, the surviving spouse receives an annual allowance equal to 60 per cent of the basic pension. Each dependent child receives an annual allowance equal to 10 per cent of the basic pension (the total for all dependent children not to exceed 30 per cent of the basic pension). If there is no surviving spouse, each dependent child receives 20 per cent of the basic pension (the total not to exceed 80 per cent of the basic pension). A dependent child is defined as someone under the age of 21 or between the ages of 21 and 25 and attending a post-secondary institution.

- Former members' pensions are increased to reflect increases in the cost of living once a member has attained the age of 60, or earlier if the member is disabled. Pensions paid to a surviving spouse, child or orphan are indexed immediately. At this point, the pension is adjusted to reflect changes in the accumulated cost of living since the year of retirement and is indexed annually thereafter.
- If a person ceases to be a member (or dies) before contributing to the pension plan for at least six years, a lump sum, called a withdrawal allowance, is paid to the person (or estate); the allowance is equal to the total amount of contributions paid by the former member, plus the interest on those contributions at a rate of four per cent per year.
- If a former member receiving a pension is re-elected to the House of Commons or appointed to the Senate, pension payments are suspended.
- Retired Members of Parliament who earn more than $5,000 a year from an appointment, employment, or a personal service contract in the federal public sector after July 13, 1995 have their pensions reduced by the amount of their earnings in excess of $5,000. The federal public sector includes Crown corporations, federal agencies, the judiciary, the diplomatic corps, and the public service.
- Participation in the plan was optional for members of the House of Commons in the 35th parliament. Effective in the 36th parliament, participation in the plan is mandatory, as it was in earlier parliaments.

Travel-Related Allowances

Travel Status Expenses

Members receive 64 travel points per year, to be used for travel on parliamentary business. One travel point is the equivalent of one first-class return trip to any destination in Canada. Under certain conditions, members can allocate their points to their employees, spouses and dependants.

Travel Status Allowance

Members are entitled to claim reimbursement for accommodation costs, meals and incidental expenses they incur while travelling on parliamentary business more than 100 kilometres from their principal residence. An annual maximum on these expenses is set by the Board of Internal Economy of the House of Commons. The amount currently allotted is $6,000. Members and their spouses, dependants and employees can also claim reimbursement for parking and local ground transportation expenses incurred in travelling to and from train terminals, airports, etc.

Constituency Travel Expenses

Members or persons representing the member can be reimbursed for travel costs to meet expenses incurred while travelling within the constituency or within the province or territory in which the constituency is situated. Receipts must be submitted, and the amount reimbursed is deducted from the member's office budget.

Services Provided

Telephone

The House of Commons covers the cost of local and long-distance calls from the member's constituency office and Parliament Hill office.

Printing

The House of Commons covers the cost of printing newsletters sent by the member to all constituents up to four times a year and brochures delivered to no more than ten per cent of the households in the constituency an unlimited number of times per year.

Office Supplies

Office supplies for members' Parliament Hill and constituency offices are provided by the House of Commons.

Office Equipment

The House of Commons provides furniture, computer equipment, software and renovations for the member's Parliament Hill office. Furniture, equipment, software and renovations for the constituency office are paid for from the member's office budget.

Payment of GST/HST

The GST and HST related to items charged to the member's office budget are paid by the House of Commons and charged to a government-wide account, not the member's budget.

Mail

Mail sent by or addressed to a member of the House of Commons can be transmitted to or from any point in Canada free of postage. Members also have at their disposal an integrated system of internal mail, distribution and messenger services to facilitate the movement of correspondence, parcels, parliamentary documents, etc.

Severance Allowance

A former member (or the member's estate if the member dies in office) who is not entitled to a pension is entitled to a severance allowance equal to 50 per cent of the total of
- the sessional allowance to which the member was entitled as of the day before the election (or at the time of death); and
- any salary or allowance payable to members occupying certain offices or positions such as minister of the Crown.

The severance allowance is also payable to a member of the House of Commons who resigns because of a permanent illness or infirmity that, in the opinion of the Speaker of the House of Commons, prevents the member from performing his/her duties. However, a severance allowance is not payable to a member who resigns for any reason other than this or to whom an allowance is payable under the *Members of Parliament Retiring Allowances Act.* The severance allowance is in addition to any withdrawal allowance that may be payable.

Resettlement Provisions

A former member who is not re-elected is entitled to a one-time reimbursement of resettlement expenses incurred within a year of the former member leaving office, for services in Canada related to financial, retirement, re-employment or stress management counselling, outplacement, education or training. The amount reimbursed by the House of Commons for these purposes is not to exceed $9,000 plus any portion transferred in from the winding-up provisions (explained below), if applicable. This provision is not available to a member who resigns.

For purposes of resettlement, a former member can claim reasonable travel expenses for up to four trips in Canada (economy class, without stopover). In making a claim, a former member must provide receipts and certify the purpose for which these expenses were incurred.

Winding-Up Provisions

A former member who is not re-elected is entitled to reimbursement of expenses incurred, such as storage and temporary help, as directed by the Board of Internal Economy, related to winding up the former member's parliamentary functions and offices. The expenses must be incurred within the three months of the individual ceasing to be a member, and up to $9,000 in expenses can be reimbursed. Any unused portion of this provision can be applied to supplement the services described earlier under *Resettlement Provisions.* This provision is not available to a member who resigns or does not seek re-election.

The travel provisions available to members who do not seek re-election under the resettlement provisions also apply under the winding-up provisions.

Removal

Once during each parliament, and on production of receipts, a member can be reimbursed actual and reasonable expenses incurred in moving the member, the member's spouse and dependants, and their personal and household effects from the member's residence to a residence in or near the National Capital Region and back to any place in Canada.

Insurance

Members of Parliament are eligible for the Public Service Health Care Plan, a private plan sponsored by the Government of Canada for the benefit of federal public service employees, members of the Canadian Forces, the RCMP, members of the House of Commons and the Senate, federal judges, employees of a number of designated agencies and corporations, and persons receiving pensions based on service in one of these capacities.

Supplementary life insurance, disability insurance and additional hospital coverage are available at the member's expense.

Travel insurance of $250,000 for members and $350,000 for ministers (whether or not they are travelling on official business) is provided; partial coverage for spouses and dependent children is provided only for official business travel.

Flight insurance of $300,000 is provided for members, family and staff for flights taken on any carrier where the airline ticket is issued by the House; the amount of coverage can be increased to $1,000,000 at the member's option and expense.

Members' Budgetary Framework[1]
The Office Budget

Each member is entitled to an office budget, to be used as directed by and subject to the conditions set by the Board of Internal Economy. The Comptroller's Office verifies that all expenses charged to a member's budget have been incurred in accordance with the rules prescribed by the Board.

The amount of the budget allotted to a member depends on the type of constituency (rural or urban). Members representing constituencies that include more than 70,000 electors and/or are more than 8,000 square kilometres in area are entitled to budgetary supplements ranging from $5,380 to $32,220. In 1997-98, office budgets ranged from $172,700 to $207,920, with the average member's budget, including supplements, being $176,592.

The office budget covers staff salaries and other expenses related to a member's office on Parliament Hill. The budget must also cover staff, office rental, telephone and other utilities, furniture, equipment, and supplies for the constituency office(s).

A member has full discretion in directing and controlling work performed on the member's behalf by employees and independent contractors and is subject only to the authority of the Board of Internal Economy and the House of Commons in exercising that discretion. For example, a member can recruit, hire, promote and release employees and determine their duties, their hours of work, and their job classifications and salaries. Employee relations are the member's responsibility. A member can appoint any number of employees (within budgetary constraints) and pay any salary up to the maximum prescribed by the Board of Internal Economy (currently $60,460).

The office budget is also used to reimburse transportation expenses incurred when the member travels within the province or territory in which the constituency is located.

---

1   The member's office budget was not part of the Commission's mandate but is described here to provide a full picture of the resources at members' disposal.

Members' Office Budget:
Average Expenditure Pattern
Actual, 1995-96

Item	$	%
Salaries Ottawa and Constituency Office	128,708	72.9
Service Contracts Research, office staff, householder preparation	6,122	3.5
Constituency Travel In constituency and in province or territory of constituency	6,481	3.7
Leases Constituency offices, office and other equipment	15,857	9.0
Constituency Office Telephone Local service, equipment rental and long- distance calls not chargeable to central account	4,938	2.8
Constituency Office Operating Costs Stationery and office supplies not charged to central account Computer software Janitorial services Insurance and security services Other utilities Subscriptions and publications Miscellaneous	8,146	4.6
Constituency Office Furniture and Equipment	2,382	1.3
Advertising Office hours, locations and meetings	3,468	1.9
Miscellaneous Expenses	490	0.3
Total	176,592	100

Remuneration and Benefits for Members of the Senate

Like members of the House of Commons, members of the Senate receive a sessional indemnity set by the *Parliament of Canada Act* and, in the absence of the current freeze, adjusted annually under the formula described earlier.

Sessional Indemnity

Like that of members of the House of Commons, the sessional indemnity of senators is frozen at the 1991 level of $64,400 until December 31, 1997.

Eligibility for payment of the sessional indemnity and the incidental expense allowance commences on the date of a senator's appointment. In the event of death, the sessional indemnity is paid to the end of the month in which death occurs, and the expense allowance is paid up to and including the day of death.

Incidental Expense Allowance

Senators receive an expense allowance of $10,100, also set by the *Parliament of Canada Act* and also frozen at the 1991 level until December 31, 1997. This allowance is not subject to income tax, nor is it necessary to provide receipts to document expenses.

Attendance and Deductions for Non-Attendance

Section 65(1) of the *Parliament of Canada Act* requires monthly attendance statements from senators, while sections 57(1) and 63(4) provide for deductions of $60 from the sessional allowance and $60 from the expense allowance for each day beyond 21 on which a senator does not attend a sitting of the Senate.

For purposes of such deductions, each day during a session on which
* the senator did not attend the Senate because of public or official business;
* there was no sitting of the Senate because it adjourned for that day; or
* the senator was unable to attend because of illness
is considered a day of attendance by the senator at that session.

Retirement Benefits

The *Members of Parliament Retiring Allowances Act,* introduced in 1952 to provide pension coverage for members of the House of Commons, was extended to cover most senators in June 1965. Participation in the plan is mandatory for members of the Senate appointed after that date.

The act stipulates the following in respect of members of the Senate:
* Senators contribute 7 per cent of their sessional indemnity. (Contributions are not withheld from the incidental expense allowance.) Contributions are used to purchase further pensionable service credits and increase the retiring allowance payable.
* Senators receiving an additional indemnity for extra duties such as a leader of the government in the Senate, deputy leader, whip, etc. have the option of contributing up to 9 per cent of these amounts as well.

- A minimum of six years of service as a senator is needed to be eligible for a pension. Pensions are paid at the rate of 3 per cent per year of service based on the average of the best six years of earnings. Pensions are limited to a maximum of 75 per cent of pre-retirement earnings (after 25 years).
- A pension is payable to a former senator at age 55, or earlier if the former senator is disabled. In the event of the death of a senator or former senator, the surviving spouse receives an annual allowance equal to 60 per cent of the basic pension. Each dependent child receives an annual allowance equal to 10 per cent of the basic pension (however, the total for all dependent children is not to exceed 30 per cent of the basic pension). If there is no surviving spouse, each dependent child receives 20 per cent of the basic pension (the total not to exceed 80 per cent of the basic pension).
- Senators' pensions are increased to reflect increases in the cost of living once the pensioner attains the age of 60, or earlier if the pensioner is disabled. Pensions paid to a surviving spouse, child or orphan are indexed immediately. At this point, the pension is adjusted to reflect changes in the accumulated cost of living since the year of retirement and is indexed annually thereafter.
- If a person ceases to be a senator (or dies) and has not contributed to the pension plan for at least six years, a lump-sum withdrawal allowance is paid to the person (or the estate), equal to the total amount of contributions paid by the former senator, plus interest on those contributions at a rate of 4 per cent per year.
- If a former senator who is receiving a pension is elected to the House of Commons, pension payments are suspended.
- Retired senators who earn more than $5,000 a year from an appointment, employment, or personal service contract in the federal public sector accepted after July 13, 1995 have their pensions reduced by the amount of their earnings in excess of $5,000 annually. The federal public sector includes Crown corporations, federal agencies, the judiciary, the diplomatic corps, and the public service.
- Pensions paid under the *Members of Parliament Retiring Allowances Act* can be attached to honour family support orders and are subject to division on marriage breakdown, as provided under the *Pension Benefits Division Act*.

Travel-Related Entitlements

Section 63(1) of the *Parliament of Canada Act* provides for the reimbursement of transportation and travelling expenses for senators. For practicality and equity, travel entitlements are administered through a travel point system. Each senator is allowed up to 64 points per calendar year for travel on parliamentary business, each point representing one round-trip to any destination in Canada. Points can be used by senators and their staff, spouses and dependent children.

First-class travel was eliminated in May 1992; reimbursement cannot exceed business-class airfare.

Hospitality expenses are not reimbursed.

Removal

Once during a parliamentary career, senators can be reimbursed, on production of receipts, the actual and reasonable expenses incurred in moving the senator, the senator's spouse and dependants, and their personal and household effects to and from Ottawa.

Insurance

Supplementary life insurance is available at the senator's expense (the benefit is twice the sessional indemnity and incidental expense allowance).

The government pays 50 per cent of provincial (Alberta and B.C.) health insurance premiums for senators resident in those provinces.

Travel insurance of $250,000 is provided for senators (whether or not they are travelling on official business), and partial coverage is provided for spouses and dependent children only when travelling on official business.

Death Benefit

In the event of the death of a senator, a death benefit equal to two months of the sessional indemnity is payable to the surviving spouse or to the estate.

History of Remuneration for Members of the House of Commons

> The reason I sought public office was to give something back to the community. Yet the work of parliamentarians, who enter public life at great cost to their professional and private lives, is rarely accepted for what it is, and many times is seen in a negative light.[2]

Practices surrounding compensation for Members of Parliament for their service to Canada's parliamentary business have varied throughout history. Introduction of the sessional indemnity in 1867 was designed to compensate these part-time members for losses incurred while they were in Ottawa, away from their homes and ordinary way of earning a living. The idea of membership in the House of Commons being a part-time job declined as the length of parliamentary sessions increased, and as the sessions lengthened and members' responsibilities grew, sessional indemnities rose as well. A pension plan for members was established in 1952, and by 1953, the job was well on the way to being considered a full-time occupation: the amount of the indemnity no longer depended on the length of a session, and members started to receive an annual salary, paid monthly.

Over the years, amendments to the *Members' Indemnity Act* reflected this change in the nature and scope of parliamentary business. Today's indemnities and allowances are the result of 24 successive amendments to the *Members' Indemnity Act* and its successor statutes.

Evolution of the Sessional Indemnity

In 1867, parliamentary business required each member of the House of Commons and the Senate to sacrifice between three and five weeks each year to tend to the nation's needs (see Appendix, Duration of Sessions of Parliament). For this service to their country, the *Members' Indemnity Act* of 1867 provided a sessional indemnity of $600

---

2   Speech by the Honourable Gilbert Parent, Speaker of the House of Commons, to the Canadian Club of Calgary, 19 January 1996.

for each session that extended beyond 30 days. This indemnity was payable at an interim daily rate of $4. Any of the $600 that remained unpaid at the daily rate was paid at the end of the session. For sessions of 30 days or less, each member of the Senate and the House of Commons received a per diem allowance of $6. This was not considered a salary but was intended to compensate for lost income from private-sector employment or a profession.

In 1873 the sessional indemnity was increased to $1,000, and the daily rate for sessions of 30 days or less was revised to $10. In 1886, the *Members' Indemnity Act* was incorporated into the *Senate and House of Commons Act*. At that time, the interim daily rate for sessions extending beyond 30 days was raised to $7. According to the preamble to the act, the indemnity was raised to reflect longer sessions and increases in the cost of living.

The sessional indemnity was raised to $1,500 in 1901, but the daily rate for sessions that did not extend beyond 30 days remained at $10.

In 1905, the maximum sessional indemnity was adjusted to $2,500. The interim daily rate for sessions that extended beyond 30 was increased to $10, and the daily rate for sessions lasting not more than 30 days was increased to $20.

In 1920, the sessional allowance was adjusted to $4,000 and the minimum duration for which a sessional indemnity was payable was extended from 30 to 50 days. The per diem rate for sessions not extending beyond 50 days was raised to $50.

The minimum duration was increased again in 1923, from 50 to 65 days. The interim daily rate for sessions lasting more than 65 days was raised to $20, but the per diem rate for sessions not extending 65 days remained at $25.

In 1945, a new allowance was introduced: members of the House of Commons and the Senate received an allowance of $2,000 for expenses incidental to the discharge of their duties as members. The allowance was payable at the end of the calendar year and was subject to deductions in respect of non-attendance at sittings. The allowance was taxable in the case of ministers of the Crown, senators, and the leader of the opposition in the House of Commons, but not in the case of members of the House of Commons.

The sessional basis for remuneration was discontinued in 1953, to be replaced by annual remuneration, although the name did not change. A sessional indemnity of $8,000 per year was payable in monthly installments on the last day of each month, while the incidental expense allowance of $2,000 per year, established in 1945, was made payable quarterly.

In 1963, the sessional indemnity was increased to $12,000, the incidental expense allowance was raised to $6,000 for members of the House of Commons, and the tax exemption on the expense allowance was extended to members of both chambers.

The sessional indemnity was raised again in 1971, to $18,000, and the incidental expense allowance rose to $8,000. This increase was attributable mainly to the recommendations of the Advisory Committee to Review Members' Allowances, appointed by the government in 1970. The committee reviewed the financial arrangements for senators and members of the House of Commons, including both the sessional indemnity and the incidental expense allowances, and recommended the changes it considered appropriate.

Between 1974 and 1991, the sessional indemnity and the incidental expense allowance were raised on January 1 each year (or, on two occasions, twice in a year on the recommendation of a commission appointed to review the allowances). Increases were suspended for two years beginning in 1975 and, as explained earlier, allowances have been frozen since 1991.

History of Remuneration for
Members of the House of Commons

Year	Sessional Indemnity[1]	Incidental Expense Allowance[1]
1963	$12,000	$ 6,000
1971	$18,000	$ 8,000
1974	$24,000	$10,600
1977	$25,500	$11,300
1978	$26,900	$12,000
1979	$28,600	$12,700
1980	$30,600	$13,500
	$40,200[2]	
1981	$43,800	$14,700
1982	$46,400	$15,500
	$48,600	$16,300[3]
1983	$50,300	$16,800
1984	$52,800	$17,600
1985	$54,600	$18,200
1986	$56,100	$18,700
1987	$57,400	$19,100
1988	$58,300	$18,300
1989	$60,000	$19,900
1990	$62,100	$20,600
1991	$64,400	$21,300

1   Current dollars.
2   As recommended by the McIsaac-Balcer commission, members' annual sessional indemnity was raised on 1 July 1980 as well.
3   The second increase in 1982 was the result of report of the McIsaac-Balcer commission, which recommended a phased approach to increases.

History of Remuneration for Members of the Senate

The history of senators' remuneration follows roughly the same path as that of members of the House of Commons, although the precise amounts of the sessional indemnity and incidental expense allowance available to senators and members of the House of Commons have differed somewhat on occasion.

History of Remuneration for Senators

Year	Sessional Indemnity[1]	Incidental Expense Allowance[1]
1963	$12,000	$3,000
1971	$18,000	$4,000
1974	$24,000	$5,300
1977	$25,500	$5,600
1978	$27,000	$5,900
1979	$28,700	$6,200
1980	$30,700	$6,600
	$40,200	$7,000[2]
1981	$32,800	$7,000
1982	$46,400	$7,600
	$48,800	$7,900[3]
1983	$50,300	$8,200
1984	$52,800	$8,800
1985	$54,600	$8,800
1986	$56,100	$9,000
1987	$57,400	$9,200
1988	$58,300	$9,300
1989	$60,000	$9,500
1990	$62,100	$9,800
1991	$64,400	$10,100

---

1   Current dollars.

2   As recommended by the McIsaac-Balcer commission, members' annual sessional indemnity was raised on 1 July 1980 as well.

3   The second increase in 1982 was the result of report of the McIsaac-Balcer commission, which recommended a phased approach to increases.

Impact of the 1991 Freeze

The sessional indemnity and incidental expense allowance of Members of Parliament have been frozen at their 1991 levels since 1992. The accompanying table shows what the sessional indemnity and expense allowance would have been if the freeze had not been in effect and the indemnity and allowance had been adjusted in line with the formula provided in the *Parliament of Canada Act.*

Impact of the 1991 Freeze on the Sessional Indemnity and the Incidental Expense Allowance for Members of the House of Commons

	Consumer Price Index		Industrial Product Price Index (Industrial Aggregate)		Projected Indemnity	Projected Allowance
Year	Index	% increase over previous year	Index	% increase over previous year		
1991	126.2	5.6	124.5	4.6	$64,400	$21,300
1992	128.1	1.5	128.9	3.5	$66,720	$22,070
1993	130.4	1.8	131.2	1.8	$67,050	$22,180
1994	130.7	0.2	133.7	1.8	$67,590	$22,360
1995	133.5	2.2	134.9	1.0	$67,590	$22,360
1996	135.6	1.6	137.8	2.1	$67,590	$22,360

Note: Under the statutory formula, changes in the indemnity and expense allowance are calculated as the change in the Consumer Price Index or the change in the Industrial Aggregate minus 1 per cent, which ever is less, so in years of low inflation, there might be no adjustment (see 1995).
Source: House of Commons, Financial Services.

Appendix
Duration of Sessions of Parliament
1867-1997

Parliament	Session	Dates	Duration of Session (days)	Number of Senate Sittings	Number of Commons Sittings
First (1867-1872)	First	1867-1868	199	75	83
	Second	1869	69	43	49
	Third	1870	87	57	62
	Fourth	1871	59	39	43
	Fifth	1872	65	41	46
Second (1873)	First	1873	161	49	59
	Second	1873	16	9	11
Third (1874-1878)	First	1874	62	39	42
	Second	1875	64	47	48
	Third	1876	63	41	46
	Fourth	1877	80	54	59
	Fifth	1878	93	59	67
Fourth (1879-1882)	First	1879	92	58	64
	Second	1880	86	56	57
	Third	1880-1881	103	55	65
	Fourth	1882	98	62	68
Fifth (1883-1886)	First	1883	107	61	73
	Second	1884	94	56	67
	Third	1885	173	88	119
	Fourth	1886	98	52	65
Sixth (1887-1890)	First	1887	72	37	49
	Second	1888	90	50	61
	Third	1889	92	53	65
	Fourth	1890	121	67	81
Seventh (1891-1896)	First	1891	155	78	102
	Second	1892	136	66	87
	Third	1893	66	37	47
	Fourth	1894	131	73	87
	Fifth	1895	96	54	65
	Sixth	1896	111	55	70

Parliament	Session	Dates	Duration of Session (days)	Number of Senate Sittings	Number of Commons Sittings
Eighth (1896-1900)	First	1896	48	28	34
	Second	1897	97	51	65
	Third	1898	131	68	86
	Fourth	1899	149	78	102
	Fifth	1900	168	77	115
Ninth (1901-1904)	First	1901	107	54	73
	Second	1902	90	43	63
	Third	1903	227	98	155
	Fourth	1904	154	66	103
Tenth (1905-1908)	First	1905	191	68	129
	Second	1906	128	67	88
	Third	1906-1907	157	62	95
	Fourth	1907-1908	236	89	148
Eleventh (1909-1911)	First	1909	120	49	84
	Second	1909-1910	175	68	102
	Third	1910-1911	255	70	117
Twelfth (1911-1917)	First	1911-1912	139	51	75
	Second	1912-1993	198	64	111
	Third	1914	148	66	103
	Fourth	1914	5	5	5
	Fifth	1915	71	37	51
	Sixth	1916	127	59	88
	Seventh	1917	246	75	135
Thirteenth (1918-1921)	First	1918	68	38	47
	Second	1919	138	62	93
	Third	1919	71	32	50
	Fourth	1920	127	54	86
	Fifth	1921	111	55	79
Fourteenth (1922-1925)	First	1922	113	44	75
	Second	1923	151	63	98
	Third	1924	143	60	95
	Fourth	1925	143	50	98
Fifteenth (1926)	First	1926	177	42	111

Parliament	Session	Dates	Duration of Session (days)	Number of Senate Sittings	Number of Commons Sittings
Sixteenth (1926-1930)	First	1926-1927	127	34	54
	Second	1928	138	52	93
	Third	1929	128	44	83
	Fourth	1930	100	28	62
Seventeenth (1930-1935)	First	1930-1931	15	11	12
	Second	1931	145	50	96
	Third	1932	113	42	78
	Fourth	1932-1933	234	64	119
	Fifth	1934	1601	59	105
	Sixth	1935	170	57	97
Eighteenth (1936-1940)	First	1936	139	49	91
	Second	1937	87	37	87
	Third	1938	156	61	102
	Fourth	1939	143	47	103
	Fifth	1939	7	6	6
	Sixth	1940	1	1	1
Nineteenth (1940-1945)	First	1940	174	42	61
	Second	1940-1942	441	34	105
	Third	1942-1943	371	38	124
	Fourth	1943-1944	364	52	120
	Fifth	1944-1945	371	62	136
	Sixth	1945	29	13	19
Twentieth (1945-1949)	First	1945	104	44	76
	Second	1946	171	72	118
	Third	1947	169	59	115
	Fourth	1947-1948	209	69	119
	Fifth	1949	95	39	59
Twenty-first (1949-1953)	First	1949	87	43	64
	Second	1950	135	65	90
	Third	1950-1951	154	14	17
	Fourth	1951	253	62	105
	Fifth	1951	82	36	56
	Sixth	1952	267	60	87
	Seventh	1952-1953	176	59	108

Parliament	Session	Dates	Duration of Session (days)	Number of Senate Sittings	Number of Commons Sittings
Twenty-second (1953-1957)	First	1953-1954	227	77	139
	Second	1955	203	79	140
	Third	1956	218	78	152
	Fourth	1956-1957	44	5	5
	Fifth	1957	95	46	71
Twenty-third (1953-1958)	First	1957-1958	111	45	78
Twenty-forth (1958-1962)	First	1958	117	59	93
	Second	1959	185	75	127
	Third	1960	210	87	146
	Fourth	1960-1961	316	91	174
	Fifth	1962	91	40	65
Twenty-fifth (1962-1963)	First	1962-1963	132	43	72
Twenty-sixth (1963-1965)	First	1963	220	78	117
	Second	1964-1965	411	106	248
	Third	1965	157	23	53
Twenty-seventh (1966-1968)	First	1966-1967	476	117	250
	Second	1967-1968	352	62	155
Twenty-eighth (1968-1972)	First	1968-1969	406	97	197
	Second	1969-1970	350	84	155
	Third	1970-1972	497	138	244
	Fourth	1972	198	47	91
Twenty-ninth (1973-1974)	First	1973-1974	419	110	206
	Second	1974	72	31	50
Thirtieth (1974-1979)	First	1974-1976	744	216	343
	Second	1976-1977	371	103	175
	Third	1977-1978	358	93	151
	Fourth	1978-1979	167	66	98
Thirty-first (1979)	First	1979	67	31	49

Parliament	Session	Dates	Duration of Session (days)	Number of Senate Sittings	Number of Commons Sittings
Thirty-second (1980-1984)	First	1980-1983	1326	329	591
	Second	1983-1984	215	54	116
Thirty-third (1984-1988)	First	1984-1986	662	159	308
	Second	1986-1988	761	194	389
Thirty-fourth (1988-1993)	First	1988-1989	79	7	11
	Second	1989-1991	770	149	308
	Third	1991-1993	850	160	271
Thirty-fifth (1994-1997)	First	1994-1996	763	133	283
	Second	1996-1997	426	96	164

The Compensation of Canadian
Parliamentarians Compared with that of
Provincial and Territorial Legislators,
Selected World Legislators, and
Senior Federal Public Servants

RESEARCH
PAPER 3

CONTENTS

Research Paper 3

The Compensation of Canadian Parliamentarians Compared with that of Provincial and Territorial Legislators, Selected World Legislators, and Senior Public Servants

This paper provides a comparative overview of the salaries of legislators in Canada and around the world, as well as information on the pension arrangements in place for legislators elsewhere in the world and a look at the salaries of senior public servants and governor-in-council appointees in Canada.

Salaries in World and Canadian Legislatures

The accompanying tables set out the current salaries of members of selected legislatures in Canada and around the world. In the first table, our comparisons are with nations with which we have much in common. They are western liberal democracies and are generally prosperous, many are G7 members, some belong to the Commonwealth, and all have vigorous national legislatures. The second table provides the figures for sessional indemnities and expense allowances in the federal, provincial and territorial legislatures of Canada.

Salaries of Members in Selected Legislatures Around the World
as of October 1997

Legislature	Salary ($ Canadian*)
Japan	$196,759
United States	$185,704
France	$121,754
Germany	$111,292
England	$96,455
Australia	$80,433
Norway	$77,640
New Zealand	$65,619
Canada	**$64,400**
Sweden	$61,666

* Figures include salary only; expense allowances, common to many of the legislatures, are not included. Converted from the original currency using figures provided by the Bank of Canada in October 1997.
Source: Information gathered by the Reference Section, Library of Parliament.

Salaries and Allowances in
Federal, Provincial and Territorial Legislatures
as of October 1997

Legislature	Base Salary	Incidental Expense Allowance	% Increase since 1981
Canada	$64,400	$21,300	47
Alberta	$36,420	$18,210	65
British Columbia	$32,812	$16,406	25
Manitoba*	$56,500	—	218**
New Brunswick	$35,735	$14,294	65
Newfoundland	$38,028	$19,014	178
Northwest Territories	$36,748	$ 1,000	182
Nova Scotia	$30,130	$15,065	87
Ontario*	$78,000	—	160**
Prince Edward Island	$29,600	$ 8,973	131
Quebec	$63,469	$11,392	92
Saskatchewan	$38,546	$ 7,622	227
Yukon	$30,38	$15,416	64

* Ontario and Manitoba abolished the incidental expense allowance and gave their members an increase in the base salary.
** Increases reflect abolition of the incidental expense allowance and its inclusion in the base salary.
Source: Fleming's Canadian Legislatures, 1997 edition.

World Legislators' Pensions[1]

Norway

Former members of the legislature are entitled to a pension when they reach the age of 65. After 12 years of service, the member is eligible for a full pension in the amount of 66 per cent of the basic salary, which at the present is NOK 264,000 ($50,160) per annum.

---

1   Much of the information in this section was gathered by the Reference Section, Library of Parliament. The Commission is grateful for this assistance.

Sweden

The retirement pension paid to former parliamentarians constitutes a complement to Sweden's old age pension and the general supplementary pension.

The pension is based on a pensionable income made up of an average of members' salaries, together with any fixed extra allowances, during the last five years before retirement. The retirement pension is 11.5 per cent of this amount up to 7.5 times the basic price index (the limit for the general supplementary pension) and 65 per cent of anything over that amount. The minimum amount of service required to receive a pension is 6 years, and members must have reached the age of 50. To receive a full pension, a member must have had at least 12 years of service.

Members not entitled to a pension, but who have served at least three years before reaching age 65, receive a life annuity. A member who resigns before the age of 65 and after at least 3 years of continuous service is entitled to a guaranteed income (that is, the parliament guarantees a former member a certain level of monthly income).

France

The pensions of members of the National Assembly are funded through contributions deducted from the members' sessional indemnity and a grant from the Assembly's annual budget.

Pensions are calculated on the basis of the number of annual contributions made.

Members are entitled to collect a pension at age 55. That age is lowered to 50 for former members of the Resistance and former political internees or deportees.

The average member's annual gross pension is currently 14,931 francs a month ($41,406 per year, as of October 1997).

Australia

According to the Australian finance department, "The Parliamentary Contributory Superannuation Act, 1948 provides a contributory superannuation scheme under which benefits are paid to former Members of Parliament, their spouses and orphan children. Membership in the scheme is compulsory. The Parliamentary Contributory Superannuation Scheme is administered under the direction of the Parliamentary Retiring Allowances Trust which consists of five trustees, the Minister of Finance and two Senators and two Members of the House of Representatives appointed by their respective Houses."[2]

Contributions

Contributions are paid to the Consolidated Revenue Fund. Contributions by senators and members of the House of Representatives are a fixed percentage of
(a) The backbench salary payable from time to time. For senators and members whose period of parliamentary service is less than 18 years, the rate of

---

2   Department of Finance, Parliamentary Contributory Superannuation Scheme Handbook (Canberra: July 1997), p. 1.

contribution is 11.5 per cent of the monthly amount of the backbench salary. Once a senator or member has completed 18 years service, the contribution rate declines to 5.75 per cent.

(b) Any additional salary, or allowance in the nature of salary, received from time to time for service as prime minister, a minister or office-holder in parliament. Senators and members who have not attained their maximum additional pension entitlements are required to pay, in addition to regular contributions at the rate of 11.5 per cent, 11.5 per cent of the additional salary received. For senators and members who have attained their maximum additional pension entitlement, the contribution rate declines to 5.75 per cent while that maximum applies. The contributions cease to be payable when the additional salary ceases to be received.[3]

Period of Service

For purposes of determining entitlements under the pension plan, period of service means the period during which the senator or member was entitled to receive a salary. Members and senators are generally entitled to a pension after 12 years of service, but may be entitled after 8 years under certain circumstances.

Benefits Payable

Retired members of the Senate and the House of Representatives receive pensions in amounts stated as a percentage of the backbench salary payable to members of Parliament, with the rate varying from 50 per cent after 8 complete years of service to 75 per cent after 18 complete years or more. The pension benefit of someone who has served more than 8 but less than 18 complete years is increased on a prorated basis for each additional day of service above 8 years.

Invalidity Benefits

The pension plan also includes provisions for retirement of senators or members found to unable to perform their duties because of physical or mental impairment. Where such a determination is made, the retirement is deemed to be involuntary, so pension benefits are provided if sufficient service has been achieved.

If sufficient service has not been achieved, the nature of the invalidity benefit depends on the extent of the person's incapacity in relation to non-parliamentary employment. The trust determines the percentage of incapacity having regard to criteria specified in the act.

The three classes of invalidity are as follows:
Class 1 — 60% to 100% incapacity
Class 2 — 30% to 59% incapacity
Class 3 — less than 30% incapacity

Class 1 and 2 benefits are expressed as non-commutable pensions of 50 per cent and 30 per cent of backbench salary respectively. The Class 3 benefit is 3.5 times the amount of the member's own contributions.

---

3   Department of Finance, p. 2.

Benefits for Those Not Entitled to a Pension

A senator or member who does not qualify for a pension is entitled to a lump sum payment, consisting of a refund of contributions plus a supplement:

- If retirement is involuntary, the supplement is two and one-third times the contributions paid by the person.
- If retirement is deemed voluntary, the supplement is one and one-sixth times the contributions paid during the last 8 years of service.

Lump sum benefits are increased if the minimum level of superannuation required under the superannuation guarantee has not been reached.

United States

Eligibility Requirements

General employees and congressional staff are eligible for optional retirement at 55 with 30 years of service, at age 60 with 20 years, or at age 62 with 5 years. Members of Congress are eligible for optional retirement at 55 with 30 years of service, at age 60 with 20 years, and at 62 with 5 years. They can also retire at age 60 with 10 years of service as a member and at age 50 with service in 9 congresses.[4]

Contributions and Benefit Formulas

Members contribute 8 per cent of their salary to the retirement fund.

The Civil Service Retirement System statute sets out the formulas used to calculate benefits for various groups. For members of Congress with five years of congressional service or more, the formula is 2.5 per cent of the average annual salary earned during their three consecutive highest-paid years (known as the high 3) for each year of congressional service.

When members of Congress retire before age 60, their accrued benefits are reduced by one-twelfth of one per cent for each month (one per cent a year) they are younger than 60 and one-sixth of 1 per cent for each month (two per cent a year) they are younger than 55. The reduction for members younger than 60 does not eliminate the overall advantages of their higher benefit formula; for example, a member who retires at age 55 with 30 years of service receives a benefit equal to 71.25 per cent of the high 3 rather than the 75 per cent he or she would have received without the age reduction.[5]

Early Retirement

The Civil Service Retirement System does not include separate early retirement provisions for members of Congress. The optional retirement provisions apply if a member loses an election. Members can retire early if they are 50 with 20 years of

---

4 United States General Accounting Office, Federal Retirement Benefits for Members of Congress, Congressional Staff, and Other Employees (Washington: May 1995), p. 2.

5 General Accounting Office, pp. 3-4.

service or any age with 25 years of service. Benefits are reduced by one-sixth of one per cent for each month (2 per cent a year) they are younger than 55. Members who resign or are expelled from Congress cannot receive immediate benefits unless they are at least 55 with 30 years of service, age 62 with 5 years of service, or age 60 with 10 years of service as a member.

Maximum Retirement Benefits

The maximum benefit for members of Congress (reached after 32 years of service) is 80 per cent of the greater of their high 3 or their final salary as a member of Congress. If a member leaves Congress to accept an appointment in the federal sector, the final salary of that position is used as the basis for the maximum benefit if it is greater than the former member's high 3 or final salary as a member.[6]

Re-Employment

If retired members of Congress are re-employed in either an elective or an appointed capacity, their annuities are suspended, and they participate in the system again, as if they had not retired. Re-employed retirees make contributions in the amount required for the positions they hold. On separation, they receive either
(1) reinstated annuities increased by the cost-of-living adjustments that occurred during re-employment, or
(2) recomputed annuities with credit for their additional service, regardless of the length of the re-employment.

United Kingdom

The government actuary is required by statute to make an assessment of the general financial position of the Parliamentary Contribution Pension Fund every three years. The actuary calculates two figures: the total standard contribution and the total actual contribution.

The total standard contribution is a long-term calculation. It shows the percentage of salary that, if paid throughout an MP's service, is estimated to be sufficient on average to provide the benefits of the pension plan, including full indexation. Largely as a result of improvements in the benefits provided by the plan, the total standard contribution rose from 13.5 per cent in 1972 to 23.5 per cent in 1993.

The total actual contribution is a shorter-term calculation that adjusts the total standard contribution upward or downward for an appropriate period to take account of deficits or surpluses in the fund. MPs pay a specified contribution, which was reduced from 9 per cent to 6 per cent after the actuary's 1991 recommendation. The Exchequer pays the balance of the total actual contribution, which may be higher or lower than the MPs' contributions.[7]

6　General Accounting Office, p. 7.
7　Review Body on Senior Salaries, Review of the Parliamentary Pension Scheme, Report No. 36 (London: March 1995), p. 4.

Contributions

Members must contribute 6 per cent of their salaries, while the Exchequer contributes at the rate recommended from time to time by the government actuary (currently 6.8 per cent of MPs' salaries).

Eligibility for Pensions

Retirement pensions are payable from age 65 to those who are no longer MPs. Pensions can be paid before age 65 in the following circumstances:

- subject to medical evidence, a member can be awarded an ill-health retirement pension at any age;
- an abated pension can be paid on retirement after age 50 and completion of not less than 15 years' service;
- a full accrued pension can be paid from age 60, provided service is not less than 20 years' duration, from age 61 provided that service is not less than 19 years' duration, and so on until age 64 and not less than 16 years' service. Service as a member of the Parliament of the European Communities counts toward qualifying service to the extent that it is not concurrent with service as an MP.
- Members can commute part of their pension in exchange for a capital sum of up to 1.5 times the Relevant Terminal Salary if service is 20 years or more, a lesser capital sum where service is under 20 years. The widow/ers' pension is not affected by commutation.
- A member whose prospective pension entitlement at age 65, including any retained benefits, is less than two-thirds of salary can, subject to certain conditions, purchase added years of service reckonable for pension purposes either by periodic contributions from salary or by a lump sum payment.
- A scheme to enable members to increase their pensions within Inland Revenue limits by paying additional voluntary contributions was introduced in April 1994.
- Pensions accrue at the rate of one-fiftieth of the member's salary over the last 12 months before the date of retirement for each year (pro rata for part of a year) of reckonable service since July 20, 1983 and at a rate of one-sixtieth before that date.
- Pensions are payable to the spouses of deceased MPs, subject to prescribed conditions, normally at the rate of 5/8 of the deceased member's pension or notional pension. In addition, a child's pension equal to 1/4 of the pension or notional pension is payable if there is one eligible child or 3/8 if there are two or more eligible children. The member's notional pension in the case of death in service is calculated in the same way as retirement pension (1/60 for service up to July 20, 1983, 1/50 thereafter), with reckonable service enhanced to age 65 and counted at the higher accrual rate of 1/50.[8]

---

8   Review Body on Senior Salaries, pp. 8-9.

Death Benefits

A lump sum equal to the greater of two years' salary or total unrefunded contributions with accumulated interest from the dates of payment can be paid on the death in service of an MP. In addition the spouse's and children's pensions, taken together, are augmented for the first three months up to the rate of the MP's salary at death.

Transferability

Transfers can be made from other superannuation schemes when an MP joins the parliamentary scheme; similarly, transfers can be made to other schemes when the MP leaves the House.

Increases in Pensions

Adjustments to pensions arising from changes in the cost of living are made in line with the Retail Price Index.

Salaries in the Canadian Public Sector
Governor in Council Appointments

Level of Appointment	Salary Range
GIC-1	$45,600–$53,000
GIC-2	$52,600–$62,100
GIC-3	$61,800–$72,900
GIC-4	$73,400–$86,400
GIC-5	$80,100–$94,500
GIC-6	$88,000–$103,600
GIC-7	$98,100–$115,500
GIC-8	$110,100–$129,700
GIC-9	$117,000–$142,400
GIC-10	$128,100–$155,800
GIC-11	$140,100–$170,500

Senior Federal Public Service Executives

Level of Executive	Salary Range
EX-1	$63,300–$84,000
EX-2	$79,300–$93,200
EX-3	$87,700–$103,100
EX-4	$98,700–$115,900
EX-5	$109,600–$128,900

Note: Deputy minister salaries are in the GIC-9 to GIC-11 range.
Source: Privy Council Office.

Job Content and Value

RESEARCH
PAPER 4

CONTENTS

Research Paper 4

Job Content and Value

Reasonable compensation for Members of Parliament is essential to the vitality of our parliamentary system. The St. Germain-Fox commission of 1989 put it this way:

It is essential for the health of Canada's parliamentary system that those who are most capable enter public service. To that end, Canadians must ensure that those who serve do not suffer financially and are permitted to live in reasonable comfort.[1]

An integral aspect of this "comfort" is the ability of MPs to function as autonomous individuals and focus on the issues of the day, unfettered by financial concerns beyond those considered normal for others at a similar stage of life and career development. The health of the parliamentary system and its institutions depends in significant measure on the capacity of MPs to focus on the business at hand, excluding consideration of matters extraneous to the MP's central responsibilities: representing constituents, exercising vigilance, and contributing to the public policy debate.

The purpose of this paper is to analyze the content and the value of the job of a Member of Parliament with a view to informing Commissioners' discussion of what constitutes reasonable remuneration for MPs.

How to make this evaluation? The general practice in the human resource field is to conduct either an external comparison or an internal analysis. The reliability of an external comparison depends on the degree of likeness of the work compared. The problem is that no work is the same as that of Members of Parliament. Politicians at other levels do similar work, and working in some other occupations involves similar activities, but scale, intensity and proportion are different. On the other hand, identifying job content and assigning it a value through internal analysis is necessarily a subjective exercise.

Some of the previous review commissions have attempted to identify the characteristics of MPs' work using existing methodologies for analyzing private- or public-sector jobs. The 1980 McIsaac-Balcer commission used two classification standards as a reference. The first — the requirements of the Treasury Board Classification Standard, Senior Executive Group, Executive Category — looks at requirements on the job holder to

- weigh the advantages of courses of action,
- apply authoritative knowledge,
- determine courses of action,
- gain acceptance,
- translate policy into work programs, and
- deploy resources on a long-term basis.

---

1   *Commission to Review Allowances of Members of Parliament* (St. Germain-Fox commission), (Ottawa: Supply and Services, 1989), p. xviii.

The other standard — the Classification Standard, Economics, Sociology and Statistics Group, Scientific and Professional Category — establishes a job classification by looking at

- the nature of assignments,
- the technical complexity,
- professional responsibility,
- management responsibility, and
- the impact of activities.

After applying these standards, the commission concluded that the job of an MP could best be compared to the SX-1E classification, a middle-level executive, although MPs were considered to have more responsibility.

A later review commission, the St. Germain-Fox commission, used the independent advice of Hay Management Consultants. Applying the Hay Guide Chart, which looks at know-how, problem-solving, and accountability, produced a salary figure of $78,693 as appropriate for the content of the job. By comparison, the sessional indemnity in effect at the time was $60,000.

Other commissions have compared MPs to members of other legislatures, but all such comparisons are flawed, in that the work is not actually the same. The Clarke-Campbell commission, reporting in 1985, put it this way:

> The parliamentarian's job is unique. It varies widely from jurisdiction to jurisdiction. There are no clearly established, specific standards to provide a basis of comparison. Nor are there accepted methodologies in other jurisdictions and segments of society which are readily applicable in evaluating the work of parliamentarians. Any such standards or methodologies would require considerable subjective adaptation before they could be adopted for parliamentary purposes.[2]

The alternative to using external comparisons is an internal analysis to determine the content and value of the work. Little of this type of work has been done. Canada's parliament is one of the world's most effective and successful, but surprisingly little has been written about how it works and why it functions as it does. (Some of the writing that has been done is identified at the end of this paper, along with other sources of information.)

For purposes of this paper, we identified eight main responsibilities or interest areas of MPs, the usual range of activities within those areas, and the conditions under which these activities are carried out. Each of the eight areas is considered in terms of its value or significance to Canada's governance, based on the available political science literature. To round out the study, six MPs from four political parties were canvassed for their impressions of the nature of their work in each of these areas. Their comments are interspersed with the text.

---

2   *Report of the Commission to Review Allowances of Members of Parliament* (Clarke-Campbell commission), (Ottawa: Supply and Services, 1985), p. 21.

Main Areas of Responsibility and Interest

What exactly do MPs do? It is a surprisingly complex job, and one that requires continuing attention to a wide range of subjects. A member's job is made up of eight areas of responsibility and interest:

- caucus
- constituency
- committee
- House of Commons
- portfolio
- party
- individual
- national

Each of these areas is distinct, requiring different skills and level of attention, but some or all may also overlap from time to time.

The **caucus,** a uniquely Canadian institution, is made up of members of the Senate and the House of Commons from one political party. Within each party, there may be federal, regional, and issue- or interest-based caucus groupings, each requiring scheduled meetings and other, less formal contact.

The **constituency** is the population in a defined area that elects the member to the House of Commons. The member represents everyone in the constituency — as individuals, in their dealings with government, and collectively, in terms of their local interests and their concern for the national interest.

Committees are established by Parliament for specific purposes — to consider a bill at the committee stage or to focus on a specific policy or program area. Each committee has a chair, a majority of government members, and representatives of the other parties. Committees discuss proposed legislation and may hold hearings on issues, receiving submissions from Cabinet members, public servants and members of the public.

The **House of Commons** sits a certain number of days each year, on a schedule set mainly by the government and to some extent by parliamentary business. The most familiar part of the daily sitting is Question Period, during which members recognized by the Speaker ask questions of the government, but this is only a small and not very representative portion of members' work in the House.

Opposition members may be given a **portfolio** by their caucus and thereby become the specialists for their party in that area. The portfolio may correspond to a department of government or a broader policy area, or it may focus on a region.

Political parties are formal gatherings of like-minded people, organized for the purpose of developing and promoting specific views on matters of public policy and contesting elections in the hope of forming a government.

All Members are also **individuals** with a certain standing as elected people. They are exposed to a wide range of ideas and issues through their work. Some of these hold inherent appeal for the member or relate to previous work or expertise. As well as any assigned duties, the member may work on these issues independently, including lobbying other members.

Members of Parliament are also called on to act on the **national** stage —to act not as party members or local representatives but as representatives of the country as a whole, often in their ridings and occasionally in Ottawa or abroad.

Each of these eight areas of responsibility must be balanced with the others. Life in Parliament requires both co-operation and competition, harmonious and adversarial relations, and individual, collective and national perspectives.

What is the value of this work, taken as a whole? Canada is recognized as a good place to live, with a stable government, a civil society and an educated population. Much of its quality of life is owing to the parliamentary system. Whatever Canadians may think of politicians as a group, Parliament as an institution is respected as the source and root of our prosperity and civility. To the extent that Members of Parliament contribute to the continued vitality and effectiveness of this institution, the job has considerable value.

As the St. Germain-Fox commission stated in 1989,

Parliamentarians choose the government of the country, they create its laws, they defend its sovereignty, they protect its citizens, they manage the monetary system, and they work to enhance the overall quality of life for its people. That's why public service has long been considered a noble calling.[3]

Required Activities

To reach a better understanding of its content and value, we need to consider what is involved in the MP's job. Each area of interest or responsibility has associated activities.

Caucus work involves gathering information, discussing issues with colleagues, and refining policy through debate. Considerable time is involved. In the Liberal party, for example, the national caucus meets weekly for two hours, the provincial caucuses meet for an hour a week, and the regional and special caucuses meet regularly as required. In preparation for these meetings, members will have informed themselves about the issues and discussed them among themselves and with the caucus chair.

Effective constituency work involves an education function, an ombudsman role, and a ceremonial dimension. For the first two functions, the member needs to maintain an office, and the office must be staffed most of the time. The member needs to understand public issues, problems and viewpoints and is often called upon to produce specific results for people who have asked for help. Two-way communication includes explaining party policy and actions to the public and being accountable for them. Most members hold office hours at least one day a week; for those representing constituencies outside Ottawa, this involves travel to and from Ottawa during periods when the House is sitting. For those with constitutencies distant from Ottawa, travel may consume as much as a day a week.

Constituency work varies by riding, with rural and urban ridings having different concerns. In an urban area, for example, a member may be invited to every university and community college graduation, to public meetings on issues of concern, and to community events such as parades. There are open houses, business launches,

---

3   St. Germain-Fox commission, p. xxi.

charitable events, sporting events, fairs, concerts and plays, where the member is often expected to purchase a ticket and also to speak or be recognized. Anniversaries, birthdays and funerals may require the member's presence or arrangements for messages or greetings from the Prime Minister. The member is also expected to be in the riding on public holidays like Canada Day and Remembrance Day.

With no federal ombudsman, the MP fulfils this role for constituents. The constituency and Ottawa offices handle large volumes of correspondence and phone calls, often requiring the MP's personal attention. Visits with constituents in the offices, usually on the weekends, are a regular feature. Some of this work is routine, but there are always special cases and unusual requests. As well, members often schedule events to give people a chance to meet and comment on current issues. Some members make a point of visiting every school in the riding once a year for events or classroom visits. Supporting the MP in these endeavours is a staff to run the office, manage scheduling, and maintain data bases of people met, events attended, dates to be marked, calls to be made and letters to be sent.

A member usually sits on one or two parliamentary committees. Committees hold regularly scheduled meetings in Ottawa and may also travel to receive testimony from witnesses elsewhere in the country. Meeting preparation involves reading documentation, briefs and research papers, drafting questions, developing proposals for amendments to bills, and similar tasks, depending on the nature of the committee.

As the Clarke-Campbell commission explained in its 1985 report,

> Members serve on dozens of Standing Committees, Joint Committees and Special Committees. Many Members sit on more than one of these committees. Some of the House of Commons committees and their sub-committees met more than 200 times in the course of the 32nd parliament (two of them more than 350 times).[4]

Members sit in the House of Commons on a rotating schedule, arranged with the party whip. The purpose is twofold: to maintain a quorum and to ensure that the party has enough members present in the event of an unscheduled vote. Thus, members are required to be present for defined periods, usually one or two days a week during sitting periods. One MP interviewed for this paper is obliged to be present on Tuesdays from 3:00 to 6:30 p.m. and on Fridays from 10:00 a.m. to 1:30 p.m., and this is a typical schedule.

The House of Commons is essentially a forum of adversaries: it is where opposition parties criticize government policies and propose their own alternatives, where the government explains and justifies its decision, and where the government is called to account for its actions. MPs are an essential part of this process, exposing policies and programs to public scrutiny, asking pointed questions, maintaining pressure on government to provide the answers. These activities are sometimes seen in a negative light (for example, in criticism of MPs' behaviour during Question Period), but in fact they are inherent in the parliamentary system and essential to its continued vitality.

To prepare for sittings, members study legislation, receive representations from constituents and interest groups, consider amendments, and research and prepare speeches on other matters before the House. The nature and scope of this work often

---

4   Clarke-Campbell commission, p. 6.

depends on whether the MP is a government or an opposition member and on the member's particular responsibilities within the caucus or party. Daily reading of Hansard keeps the member up-to-date with the business of the House, while attendance at the daily meeting to prepare for Question Period is essential for opposition members asking questions and others wanting to stay current with a party's House strategy.

Regardless of their particular responsibilities, members must be aware of at least the principles of proposed legislation and the party's position on it. More detailed knowledge might be required if constituents or community groups have a particular interest in a bill and make representations concerning it. As a party's critic for a particular portfolio, a member is also responsible for deciding on and proposing amendments submitted at the committee stage or in the House. As a party's subject-matter expert, a member needs to be familiar with the people, organizations and publications relevant to that area of interest and to develop an awareness of the different viewpoints.

All members are public figures and therefore potential spokespersons for their party or even for the government. They may be called upon to speak with little notice, usually about an area of expertise, but sometimes about virtually any issue of public policy. This broad general knowledge of the public agenda takes time to develop through reading and discussion.

Almost every member is elected as a member of a party. Ensuring the continued viability of the party takes continuous effort by members, party staff and volunteers. Members are in particular demand for fundraising, whether for high-profile events or at the level of individual donors.

Maintaining the party also demands continuous internal dialogue. Members need to talk with other party members about issues, understand their views, and convey their own. Members work with party officials and volunteers in the constituency. Party work also includes meetings of the local executive of the party and of the provincial and national executives. The national party meets at least twice a year.

One member described party work this way:

Political parties demand work. Networking is needed. Making contacts, trouble shooting, support, visiting, communicating, working out details, rallying the troops on an issue, are all part of team building.

Most members also maintain contact with individuals and groups that share their particular interests. Groups and individuals may stay in touch by letter and telephone, send materials, or ask a member to attend functions and make speeches. A member may become involved in lobbying other members on the issue in question. The member may deal with the public service to gain information or to promote a viewpoint. Private member's bills, press conferences, and questions on the order paper can stimulate discussion on an issue and bring attention to it.

A member is also the local representative of the country as a whole. The opening of a new office or the launch of a new program often calls for the presence of the local member. This role may also involve international work, such as the recent observation of elections in Bosnia, South Africa and Cambodia by a Canadian team. Work with parliamentary associations helps to promote international co-operation and friendship, foster the development of democratic institutions, or develop business and trade contacts.

Working Conditions

Another factor to consider in assessing the content and value of members' work is the working conditions that are inherent in the job and form the context for it.

The Clarke-Campbell commission offered this observation in 1985:

> The Commission was conscious of the fact that the complex, sensitive role of the MP requires people of considerable ability, usually at a time in their lives when their earning capacity is at its greatest. These requirements and responsibilities create a working environment that demands long hours of work and strong commitment to vital questions of public policy.[5]

As described in the preceding section, the work consists of numerous broad areas of responsibility, with widely varying activities. The job of MP also involves particular pressures:

- a heavy workload
- frequent travel
- separation from family
- life in the public eye

Workload

Describing the workload of Members of Parliament in its 1985 report, the Clarke-Campbell commission said:

> The Member from the era of Confederation would hardly recognize it as being the same role that he once played. His was a part-time job. He came to the Capital for a few months each year and was expected to carry on his normal occupation back home. He was probably a professional or businessman who could afford to take time off to make political decisions. Today, the vast majority who responded to our questionnaire consider being a parliamentarian to be a full-time job. Then, a parliamentary session might last 50 days. Today, a session may last more than twelve calendar months, and the present parliamentary calendar calls for 177 sitting days per year.
>
> For political survival in the electronic age MPs require highly developed skills as communicators. Management skills are needed to make effective use of the offices they maintain in Ottawa and their constituencies, the staff of four or more people and the budget of over $100,000 on which they operate. Add to this hundreds of public, political and social functions and it is easy to see why many MPs end up with 14-hour workdays and seven-day weeks.[6]

---

5 Clarke-Campbell commission, pp. 25-26.
6 Clarke-Campbell commission, p. 6.

MPs on the Workload[7]

Today I start with a breakfast meeting in preparation for national caucus. Question Period preparation starts at 8:00 a.m., National Caucus is from 10:00 to 12:00. There are phone calls to return and correspondence to be done, then I am speaking on a private member's bill. This evening I am the Ontario Riding Association special speaker at 6:00 p.m.

There is never a day when you can be without a function, 365 days a year. This job is for those who are dedicated. The majority really want to do something for their people; they are not here for any other reason. They are really dedicated.

The work in total involves about 90 to 95 hours a week continuously. It is incredibly complex.

People ask me to be at fairs in the village, at the 20th anniversary of the priest, at a teacher's retirement, to visit the Golden Age group, to speak at the Chamber of Commerce. I try my best to have one night free on the weekend.

The MP's long work week and constant travel would not be unfamiliar to the chief executive officer of a large corporation. But as the St. Germain-Fox commission explained in its 1989 report, the MP's conditions of employment are very different from those of a CEO:

> By the very nature of the job, Members of the House of Commons face considerable pressures: 60 to 80-hour work weeks; no job security; considerable travel, no privacy; and demands from constituents, interest groups and political parties. In addition, parliamentary life is very difficult for Members...who have a family. It is easier for those MPs with grown or no children or those who are independently wealthy. They, however, are in the minority. Most MPs are middle-income earners with families. In this, they are representative of most Canadians.[8]

An Angus Reid survey of 1500 respondents across Canada, conducted in March 1994 for the Lapointe commission, showed that people thought Members of Parliament spent between 40 and 49 hours a week on the job. In fact, according to the Sobeco Ernst & Young report of the same year, the work week is much longer:

> This represents an eleven-hour work day, six days a week when the House of Commons is in session, and a ten-hour work day, five days a week when the House is not in session. If we compare the average work schedule in Canada...and a professional's or executive's, we find that the average Member works about 500 hours more than the typical executive in Canada and 1,000 more than the average worker.[9]

---

7 Quotations set in boxes and interspersed with the text are from interviews conducted in 1997 with sitting Members of Parliament specifically for this paper.
8 St. Germain-Fox commission, p. xviii.
9 Sobeco Ernst & Young, *Parliamentarians' Compensation*, a study commissioned by the Treasury Board (Ottawa: 1994), p. 23.

Frequent Travel

Members of Parliament must be in Ottawa during periods when the House is sitting but must also make regular, usually weekly, appearances in the constituency. This involves frequent travel for all but the few MPs whose ridings are in the immediate vicinity of the National Capital Region and travel over very long distances for the MPs representing the territories and constituencies on the Atlantic and Pacific coasts. When adverse weather conditions are factored in — as they must be for five or six months each year — the extent to which MPs' time is spent preparing to travel, travelling, and recovering from travel begins to become clear.

MPs on Travel

Travel alone is the equivalent of a half-time job. There are about 20 hours of travel per week for me. As soon as you understand that the job involves both the constituency and Parliament, you understand the travel involved. Every Sunday and every Thursday I am on the plane. I average one weekend a year in Ottawa; every other weekend involves plane travel.

We specifically committed as Members to live at home and to be home. Ottawa is strictly a commute. It is physically demanding. You can end up in airports, stuck in blizzards.

Separation from Family

Previous review commissions identified the toll on family life of being a politician. The Clarke-Campbell commission observed that

> Spouses of Senators and MPs often have responsibilities related to parliamentary life. It is important that they become familiar with the workings of Parliament and their presence is sometimes required at official functions. Furthermore, public life puts family relationships under great stress which may be eased if the parliamentarians can maintain closer contact with their spouses.[10]

The McIsaac-Balcer commission (1980) said:

> For married MPs the nature of the job places an added burden on the family unit. The Member is separated from his family during the week while he is in Ottawa attending to business in the House of Commons. When the M.P. returns to his constituency on the weekend, he often sees little of his family because of the public's demands on his time. The Commission believes that MPs with families face a degree of pressure and stress that is seldom found in other occupations. One M.P. summarized his feelings this way:

---

10   Clarke-Campbell commission, pp. 37-38.

Unless you are willing to divorce your family, a family man should not become a Member of Parliament. Families suffer emotionally, sociologically, and economically. Even with subsidy from personal equity, which is rapidly depleting, my family lives at a lower standard than we did before I came to Ottawa, and my net worth is 30% lower. I will not divorce my family and therefore I will probably not run again and instead return to the community and rebuild my equity. Parliament is structured for the very young, the very old, and independently wealthy people.

Another MP said:

This has to be one of the most demanding jobs in Canada. The responsibilities are enormous; the hours punishing; and the sacrifices of your wife and family unrealistic. You know this — in a vague sort of way — before you run, but the full impact of the job has to be experienced personally before you truly understand it.[11]

MPs on Separation from Family

There is separation from family at regular times and fear of separation at crucial times in the lives of family members. You feel this especially when family members are ill or at risk, or even just at the times when someone in the family has a cold.

It has a dramatic effect on family life. There are a lot of personal sacrifices on both sides. You don't have a Saturday and a Sunday.

Life in the Public Eye

The effects of heavy workload, constant travel and family separation are compounded by the fact that almost every part of a member's life is open to public scrutiny.

The St. Germain-Fox commission summarized it this way:

The position of the Member of Parliament is quite unique and is truly stressful and demanding on those who accept these sacrifices for the privilege of serving.[12]

The Value of the Work

While it is clear that Members of Parliament are busy, what is the value of their work?

The St. Germain-Fox commission relied on the Hay Guide Chart–Profile Method of Job Evaluation, which uses three factors with eight dimensions to measure job content:

---

11   *Report of the Commission to Review Salaries of Members of Parliament and Senators*
     (McIsaac-Balcer commission), (Ottawa: Supply and Services, 1980), pp. 4-5.
12   St. Germain-Fox commission, p. xxiii.

MPs on Being in the Public Eye

On the streets in the constituency, most people recognize the member, and use the opportunity of a chance meeting to express their views on issues and comment on how the member is doing. On the other hand, you need to show you are human and that you actually live in the area.

It is true that other professions require business travel or forced absences from family, but for a member everything is public and on view. The member is on public display. It is easy to be made fun of. You need to be very open with very personal things. An operation could be the subject of speculation, so it needs to be discussed before rumours begin. The member represents a party and its philosophy, and is taken as an example of that. There is no off time.

At least one person will be against you, whatever you do, will call you, tell you about it and expect a comment from you. You need to be willing to be taught by people, but you also need to understand your principles and need to be prepared to assume a take-me-or-leave-me attitude. Not everyone will love you or be prepared for you. You need a thick skin and a sense of humour.

The member is accountable at re-election. The public persona, the press articles, all weigh in to have an impact on my ability to keep my job. You go before a pretty huge board of directors at the review time that is called election day.

Know-How. The sum total of every kind of knowledge and skill, however acquired, needed for acceptable job performance.
Problem-Solving. The amount and nature of thinking required in the job in the form of analyzing, reasoning, evaluating, creating, using judgement, forming hypotheses, drawing inferences and arriving at conclusions.
Accountability. The answerability for action and its consequences. It is the measured effect of the job on end results of the organization. It has three dimensions: freedom to act, job impact on end results, and magnitude.[13]
Using this method, Hay Management Consultants Limited determined that the salary of Members of Parliament was about 20 per cent less than that received by people doing comparable work elsewhere.
The 1994 Lapointe commission referred to the Plowden report on parliamentarians' pay and allowances in the United Kingdom, which
defined 'principal accountabilities' as 'results which need to be obtained if the job is to be performed successfully'. Six principal accountabilities were identified: 1–to provide and maintain personnel for government and opposition; 2–to monitor and criticize governments in order to influence and where possible change government action; 3–to initiate, amend and review legislation; 4–to help

---

13   St. Germain-Fox commission, p. 7.

individual constituents with specific requests; 5–to contribute to the formulation of public policy; and 6–to promote public understanding of party policies to facilitate the achievement of party objectives.[14]

Assessed using either methodology, the work of members has a great deal of value to the institution and for society as a whole. We examine the value of MPs' work in each of the eight responsibility or interest areas identified earlier.

Caucus

Discussion of issues in public between people holding different viewpoints is basic to our parliamentary system. The British parliamentarian and prime minister Benjamin Disraeli said that no government is effective without a strong opposition. In practice, this requires people to build consensus around a few ways of looking at things, then to debate these viewpoints in a public forum.

The venue for the initial discussion and consensus building is the caucus. There, members of a political party discuss in private how to apply their shared principles to a particular issue, thereby developing a position on the issue as a basis for subsequent debate in public. Without this consensus building, public debate would not be focused, and decisions could not be reached as easily. Having party caucuses speeds up decision making, makes certain that a range of viewpoints are considered, and improves the quality of public debate by defining the issues and focussing discussion productively.

Caucus discussions occur out of the public eye, ensuring that a full range of views can be heard. Party discipline is balanced by party leaders' acceptance that views are heard before a decision is reached. Elected people will not accept party discipline without its counterpart — participation in the deliberations leading to a decision or position.

Members have a great deal of latitude to speak their minds in caucus. For government members, caucus is the opportunity for MPs not in the Cabinet to make a pitch for their views or that of their constituents. In caucus, government members can ask questions and challenge ministers, something that seldom happens in the House of Commons.

Caucus has to be private, so that members feel free to speak without reservation. Without that full expression and the resulting consensus, it might not be possible for the party to move forward on the basis of consensus and solidarity. Attendance at caucus is normally obligatory. The caucus chair needs agreement on the party's basic lines of action for the coming week in order to be effective, and each member needs to know where colleagues stand and what the outcome of the discussion was.

For opposition members, caucus is an opportunity to refine ideas before presenting them in public. For new issues that do not appear in a party platform, for example, caucus is a forum for information sharing and debate, even if the issue must ultimately be referred to the party as a whole.

---

14 Commission to Review Allowances of Members of Parliament (Lapointe commission), *Democratic Ideals and Financial Realities, Paying Representatives in the 21st Century* (Ottawa: Supply and Services, 1994), p. 36.

Information dissemination is an important function of caucus. Senators and senior party officials often attend, and their experience or subject-matter expertise is valuable for members. National caucus meetings often receive reports from regional and special-interest caucuses as well. The caucus agenda normally includes new proposed legislation, as well as any outstanding issues. Where policy needs to be developed, decisions are made on what information is needed and how it is to be gathered. Occasionally, parts of proposed legislation are referred to a caucus committee for review and comment, which subsequently reports back to the full caucus.

MPs on Caucus

You see different points of view; some are worthwhile, some are not. People come to a consensus that everyone will uphold.

I spend about eight hours a week in caucus-related work.

Then there is just the need to let off steam. Problems with another MP, problems between a leader and another MP — you can say it there.

Our caucus is democratic and we elect the chair. Anything can be discussed, and anyone can speak with an equal voice. We have two rules: there is never a vote, we develop consensus; and there is no applause ever.

Caucus also serves as a reality check for ministers. The opinions of caucus allow governments to test the acceptability of policy and legislation; members have to 'sell' the policy in their ridings and know what voters will and will not accept. Proposed legislation has been changed because of caucus opposition.

Members of each party usually vote as a block in the House of Commons, but this can happen only because there was full debate in caucus. Sometimes a free vote is allowed if caucus could not reach consensus, but this is rare.

In the most recent edition of their book, *Politics in Canada: Culture, Institutions, Behaviour and Public Policy,* Jackson and Jackson note that

...governments have shown time and time again that they do not act in the face of clear caucus opposition. In 1996, Finance Minister Paul Martin, for example, gave in to caucus demands that he not amend the *Bank Act* to permit banks to sell insurance, and Human Resource Minister Doug Young was forced by caucus to propose amendments to the unemployment scheme that would have reduced the reduction for seasonal workers.

In the opposition parties, there is relatively little distinction in status between leaders and backbenchers; consequently, all MPs feel equally entitled to their point of view, and debate is often quite heated. However, even in opposition there are no formal votes and the party leader sums up the caucus consensus.[15]

---

15   R.J. Jackson and D. Jackson, *Politics in Canada: Culture, Institutions, Behaviour and Public Policy,* fourth edition (Scarborough: Prentice Hall, 1998), p. 322.

Constituency

Constituency work is a vital and valued part of the work of a Member of Parliament. There is great and increasing demand from the public for access to the MP, as an information source and as an ombudsman. Anyone who has a problem dealing with the government may come to the constituency office for help and may want to see the member in person and in private.

Writing in 1974, a former MP, Gordon Aiken, noted that

a poll [found that] looking after the problems of his constituents should be a Member's first priority. This was far ahead of any other suggestion.[16]

Reporting a decade later, the Clarke-Campbell commission observed an expansion in this role:

Members of Parliament have become virtual ombudsmen for their constituents (numbering as high as 207,803), assisting with the myriad problems which the public experiences in dealing with the mammoth bureaucracies of modern government. That, in itself, is a demanding, full-tie occupation.[17]

Political scientist C.E.S. Franks, later a member of the Lapointe commission, reinforced this point in his 1987 book, *The Parliament of Canada*:

Much of MPs' contact with their constituency, and even more of their office staff's, is involved with helping constituents with problems. This ombudsman and social-worker activity ranks very high in importance with the electorate. The Member has become an important avenue for reaching government with complaints.... This ombudsman function is relatively new. The public ranks this role very highly, more important than even the MP's role as a legislator.[18]

Constituency work involves more than assistance and problem solving. Policy ideas are of little value unless they are translated into programs with benefits for real people. To understand and appreciate the real-life effects of policies and programs, MPs need to know their constituents through contacts with a wide range of people on the full range of government programs and services.

This happens in several ways. The member seeks out the views of opinion leaders and community activists. The member participates in public meetings and other forums. The member is recognized on the street, where constituents feel free to ask questions or make comments. In these ways, the member gains a general appreciation of community views and a sense of what will and will not be acceptable. The results of these exchanges feed into caucus debate.

---

16 Gordon Aiken, *The Backbencher: Trials and Tribulations of a Member of Parliament* (Toronto: McClelland and Stewart, 1974), cited in Franks (see note 18), p. 95.
17 Clarke-Campbell commission, p. 6.
18 C.E.S. Franks, *The Parliament of Canada* (Toronto: University of Toronto Press, 1987), pp. 90-91.

MPs on Constituency Work

People are hurting these days. People expect miracles, but you can't turn them away. There are cuts in health, social programs, UC. Welfare is now so low people don't know what to do.

When I go for groceries people come up to me and comment that I am not in Ottawa, as if I am off the job. They give me a list of problems, and I walk out with my groceries and a binder full of materials. They expect follow-up right away. They want you to be in the riding or in the riding office.

There is a change. Poverty is growing, legal aid has been cut and available to fewer people. More people have no UIC and no welfare: they have lost their jobs and need to sell their property and use up the assets before they can get help.

People need someone to talk to; access to psychologists and lawyers has been cut. More and more people demand to see me in person. I tell them there is nothing I can do, but they leave relieved, because someone listened. I get questions about everything, about children, about AIDS. I get anonymous letters from people wanting help about abuse but afraid to be identified, asking me to respond in the classifieds.

For some, you feel you can help but for others you are helpless. One man had a business plan and needed $5,000 and couldn't get it. I am struck by the confidence people have — they confide in the MP. An architect, who was bankrupt, came and opened his books, with his wife there; I renegotiated with Revenue Canada to restructure the debts. You see the suffering of humanity — you do what you can.

We are intermediaries between the administration that is in place in Ottawa and the public. Our relationship with them is not partisan.... Everyone is treated alike.

I need to respond to 70 to 80 letters a day. About half require me to study and to seek out information.

Committee

Much of the work of Parliament takes place in committees. Every part of the role of the member is highlighted at the committee table. Committees can operate with a degree of independence. For example, there is more scope for a member to propose legislative amendments in committee than on the floor of the House of Commons.

In *Democratic Government in Canada,* Dawson described several aspects of Parliament's role that can be fulfilled through committee work:

> Parliament can ensure that the statutes define the discretionary areas with precision and that these areas be kept as narrow as efficient administration will

allow. Parliament can also hold the cabinet to a strict accountability for the exercise of the administrative discretionary power and can keep all such actions under its diligent scrutiny. The chief guardian against abuses is therefore an alert and even suspicious Parliament, which is encouraged and supported by public opinion fully alive to the dangerous possibilities which are always latent in modern administrative procedures. The House of Commons has now a standing committee to survey the use of delegated powers.[19]

Committees examine proposed legislation and offer a forum where both government and opposition members can propose amendments. Proposed legislation is discussed in depth by Members other than Cabinet, and flaws can be corrected by amendments, proposed either by government or opposition. Committees also review the annual estimates of departments and other financial information on the government as a whole; use annual reports as a basis for reviewing the activities of government departments; and study particular issues referred from time to time by the House of Commons.

The McIsaac-Balcer commission offered this description of the role of the House of Commons and its committees:

...to be the vigilant keeper of the public purse, to study and amend legislation in a thorough and intelligent way, to examine witnesses in a critical and detailed manner, to undertake important reviews, to study national issues, to make meaningful recommendations.[20]

MPs on Committee Work

You have to be prepared to ask questions at hearings, to do research beforehand and to be generally knowledgeable about the committee. You need to meet individuals, groups and organizations who come to see you in your capacity as committee member. When something in your area becomes a public issue, you have to handle interviews, and for this you need to be prepared and to get your facts straight.

There is negotiation among members of the committee to cover all sides, to make the debate as comprehensive as possible.

The real talent of the member is in the committees. You are alive. You ask the questions you want right away. It shows if you are informed or not. Normally the process is non-partisan.

---

19   Robert MacGregor Dawson and W.F. Dawson, *Democratic Government in Canada*, fifth edition (Toronto: University of Toronto Press, 1989), p.74.

20   McIsaac-Balcer commission, p. 55.

House of Commons

Television viewers watching proceedings in the House of Commons might agree with the travel writer, Karl Baedeker, who observed in his 1894 guidebook to Canada,

Few of the speeches delivered in the House of Commons can be called inspiring. In fact, when not personal, they are prosaic. This can hardly be helped, for a Canadian Parliament, like Congress in the United States, deals, as a rule, with matters from which only a genius could draw inspiration.

Others agree with the veteran parliamentarian, the late Stanley Knowles. During the 1956 pipeline debate, he became concerned about procedural rulings he considered a threat to Parliament. To his mind, that amounted to a threat to Canada itself:

What shall it profit Canada if we gain a pipeline, and lose a nation's soul? What shall it profit the people of Canada if we gain a thousand pipelines, and lose Parliament?

What is the value of the sittings of the House? Jackson and Jackson write that the House of Commons provides a means to limit the arbitrary power of government:

In the 32nd parliament, for example, the opposition found dramatic weapons to confront an uncooperative government. In March and April 1981, the Progressive Conservatives tied up the business of the House of Commons with a collective 'filibuster' — an apparently endless series of 'points of order' and 'questions of privilege' — in order to prevent further discussion of the resolution on patriation of the Constitution until after it had been ruled on by the Supreme Court.[21]

While television has led many people to equate the House of Commons with Question Period, the Jacksons list these elements as being vital parts of the business of the House:

The business of the House includes
- government business
- opposition business
- standing orders, opposition-requested debate on urgent issues
- orders of the day, current legislation
- oral question period
- private members' business, motions and bills
- questions on the order paper
- resolutions
- routine business
- standing orders
- urgent business[22]

---

21 Jackson and Jackson, *Politics in Canada*, p. 323.
22 Jackson and Jackson, *Politics in Canada*, p. 323.

> **MPs on House Time**
>
> All leaders develop a consensus on the agenda and on the allocation of time.
>
> All members become a family here; they spend more time with other members than they do with their own families. There is a climate of co-operation as well as of rivalry. There needs to be a consensus on the rules and their functioning. The best example is the Speaker. When he rises and chooses a person it is an agreement. Things are decided by speech rather than by fighting.

Portfolio

To ensure they function smoothly as a team, opposition parties assign 'critic', shadow cabinet, or portfolio responsibilities to ensure that at least one person in caucus focuses on each subject area, can grasp the significance of policy or legislative changes proposed by the government, and can inform or guide other caucus members, enabling them to concentrate on their own areas of responsibility.

For the official opposition, this system of assigning portfolios is also the basis of a government in waiting. When a government falls, the official opposition as a whole and some of its individual members should have the experience and the basic knowledge to begin governing.

Being the critic for a particular department or policy field involves briefings by the relevant department or departments, membership on the relevant committee, and generally staying current on the portfolio, including policy developments, program activities, and legislative change through further briefings and review of documentation.

The value of the critic's role from the perspective of Canadians is that alternative viewpoints are developed on issues in the major areas of public policy, offering greater potential for informed public debate, a more comprehensive perspective on issues, and a smoother transition between governments should that situation arise.

Party

The McIsaac-Balcer commission referred to the member's identity as a party representative:

> He also must carry out his role as a politician, articulating his party's philosophy and platform before the media and in public forums.[23]

Through the party system, individuals can find common cause with others to strengthen their voice on matters on which they are in agreement. By defining a clear viewpoint, they make debate on issues more focused, creating the potential for better decisions.

---

23 McIsaac-Balcer commission, p. 4.

MPs on Critics' Role

Any Member with a question on that issue from a constituent will come to the lead on that issue for information or to co-ordinate their activities. A party position needs to be developed on any new issues in that area. The critic will explain current events in caucus, react to suggestions of others or make suggestions, work with the leader on positions, and handle any co-ordination necessary.

As the party critic, I sit on the committee, travel on committee business, and have as many as three [related] functions a week.

Dawson and Dawson describe the role of political parties this way:

Between the formidable complexity of Canadian society and the relative simplicity of the party system found in Parliament...lie millions of man-hours of arguing, organizing, urging, bargaining, advocating and conciliating. The importance of the functions parties perform in the single-minded pursuit of their own ends can hardly be overestimated. In the first place, they have the chief responsibility for arousing interest in and educating the electorate on political matters. They also provide the organization whereby public opinion is able to add power and effectiveness to suggestion and criticism. The fact, moreover, that party members are forced to participate with many others in a joint endeavor inevitably brings about many compromises and concessions, so that resulting policy will form the highest common factor on which their conflicting interests are able to unite. Again, parties sort out and stress the major issues and they reduce the number of candidates from thirty or forty thousand eligible citizens to half a dozen or so. The task of the voter is thereby greatly simplified, and he is able to make his choice on a few questions and a few representatives of the people.

The usefulness of parties is by no means confined to the constituencies.... Parties are also indispensable to the work of cabinet and Parliament, adding to the effectiveness of the proceedings and sharpening the responsibility of both those in power and those in opposition. The party system ensures also that there will always be an alternative government available whenever the old one retires; and as its leaders and policies are well known and are prepared in advance, the transition can be made with a minimum of friction, uncertainty and delay.[24]

---

24   Dawson and Dawson, *Democratic Government in Canada*, p. 17.

> ### MPs on Party Role
>
> Within the context of the party I speak out for my constituents. Everyone will have a say, people will change their minds, and people will work in co-operation.
>
> House members need to help the party or it won't exist. There are fundraisers, annual meetings, invitations every week, receptions, CPAC programs, all representing the party. As well, there is travel for speaking at these functions.

Part of the power of party politics for members is the devotion to the shared ideas and viewpoints and a sense of their importance. This is particularly true of smaller parties. When the predecessor of the NDP, the New Party, was being formed in 1960, one member commented, "If the new party doesn't succeed, it will mean that for the next twenty-five years there'll be no left-of-centre political party in Canada."[25]

Beyond their significance to adherents, smaller parties have a value for the political process as a whole:

> Third parties, with nothing to lose, can afford to experiment with new ideas, for ideas are the only working capital they have. In the process, the public will be gradually educated to an awareness of the need for a new policy or a new program. Then, in the fullness of time, the larger parties will take over the more durable of the reforms advocated by the third parties and enact them into law.[26]

Individual

Notwithstanding party discipline, every member has the right to speak and advance his or her issues of individual interest. Private members can use motions, private member's bills and press conferences to prompt debate and put ideas into the public arena, where media attention or public concern may spread them further.

Private members' bills once had little chance of becoming law. Today, although few such bills do become law, members still have a greater chance of seeing their individual legislative proposals debated on the floor of the House and considered in committee:

> [Private members' bills] are placed in a lottery or draw. The first 30 items chosen are placed in an 'order of precedence' and the Standing Committee on Procedure and House Affairs selects up to five motions and five bills to be voted on... In September 1996, the new system worked satisfactorily, for example, to bring Bill C-216, an act to ban negative-option rules in the broadcasting legislation, to a vote.[27]

---

25   T.C. (Tommy) Douglas, remarks on the founding of the New Party, 1960 (quoted by John Robert Colombo, *Colombo's Canadian Quotations* (Edmonton: Hurtig Publishers, 1974).

26   J.R. Mallory, *The Structure of Canadian Government* (Toronto: MacMillan, 1971), p. 202.

27   Jackson and Jackson, *Politics in Canada*, p. 311.

Even if they do not become law, there is still value in the ability to submit a private member's bill for consideration by Parliament:

> Private members' bills and resolutions...serve a useful purpose. They enable a subject to be discussed and publicized and thus help educate and mobilize public opinion in their favour. When it becomes apparent that there is strong public support, it is likely that the government itself will introduce a bill on the subject. Opposition parties are often able to make skilful use of private members' time to introduce bills or resolutions which embody parts of their program, thus placing it on record and in the public eye. It would not be an exaggeration to say that practically every significant measure of reform in the last forty years has first been introduced in Parliament by a private member, usually, but not invariably, from the opposition.[28]

MPs on Individual Role

The Member needs to be a generalist and be able to give a credible three-minute speech on any subject to the media in the home riding. For this, they need to pay attention to the basics of everything that goes on and be able to comment on it. In fact, there are circumstances in which really any member could become the unofficial or even the official spokesperson for their party on any issue.

The prime minister has power over those with power or those who want it; the opposition leader over those who hope to be in cabinet. The new members follow directions, but those who are there after three elections if not in power now they will never be, and there is no means to control them, so they have power too. Individual members have more power and independence when relative standings of parties are close, or during a minority government.

Individuals can have influence over policy or orientation; they need to speak in the right place and at the right time.

In meetings of parliamentary committees, by questions, by discussion, by the guests you invite, you can contribute to the course of the decisions.

One way to live is to put into reality the subjects that are ignored by everyone else. Personality can come out in the strategy to make a subject discussed.

For motions and private members' bills, a member in our party must inform the communications department of the party, but they do not need the agreement of everyone in the caucus.

A Member is elected and has a public voice; each one has that power.

---

28   Mallory, *The Structure of Canadian Government*, p. 261.

Members of Parliament in a representative democracy are elected in the expectation that they will make decisions — some in accordance with their constituents' wishes, some in line with party policy, and some following the dictates of their conscience. With more than 300 members from different parts of the country and varying backgrounds and interests, over the long term, most issues of concern to Canadians will eventually likely have an advocate in Parliament, regardless of the views or policy of the party in power. Therein lies the importance of the individual member and the value of the work they do.

National

Members run for office as candidates for a political party, but once elected they are representatives of all the people in their constituency.

> Not lumped with 263 others in the chamber, each member is the federal presence in his own riding. He is the political authority, socially acceptable and the only one of his kind in the area.[29]

When a Member of Parliament attends social events, wedding anniversaries, official openings, annual meetings and turkey dinners, it is not so much as a member of the Conservatives, the Liberals, the NDP, the Reform Party or the Bloc Québécois as it is a Canadian public figure, someone who symbolizes the nation in a local context.

MPs on National Role

A Member represents everyone in the area. There is no partisan material in a constituency office. We represent all the people and must never forget it.

Members often travel abroad as representatives of Canada in foreign nations, for example, for peacekeeping, election observation or on trade missions.

Conclusion

"To be valuable, therefore, is to avail towards life," wrote John Ruskin in his seminal essay, Ad Valorem. "That country is richest which nourishes the greatest number of noble and happy human beings; that man is richest who, having perfected the functions of his own life to the utmost, has also the widest helpful influence, both personal, and by means of his possessions, over the lives of others."[30]

The purpose of this paper was to review the available information to arrive at a better understanding of what the work of a Member of Parliament involves and what the significance of that work is to Canada's democratic institutions and well-being as a country.

---

29   Aiken, *The Backbencher*, p. 95.
30   John Ruskin, "Ad Valorem", in *The Genius of John Ruskin: Selections from his writings*, ed. John D. Rosenberg (Boston: Houghton Mifflin, 1963), p. 270.

Other studies conducted for the commission looked at hard data on the financial remuneration assigned to the work of Members of Parliament, over time and in comparison with that received by other legislators, managers and public servants. Previous commissions compared the responsibilities and activities of MPs with those in other occupations, using standard methodologies. This paper adds a different approach to understanding, that of considering the intrinsic worth of the job of Members of Parliament, by analyzing the activities involved in the light of their potential contribution to the well-being of Canadian society. What is the full potential of the job to contribute value to the lives of individuals and of society?

Material on which to base such assessments is rarer than one might imagine. To determine what a member is responsible for, including the nature of the work, the scope of activities, the working conditions, and the value attached to this work, we considered the research and conclusions of previous commissions, reviewed the political science literature, and interviewed a number of members.

We identified several areas of responsibility in which the work done by MPs contributes to the national interest and to the health of democratic and representative institutions:

- Caucus work by members makes effective government possible because through it individual opinions and local interests can be brought to bear on discussions of the national agenda and reconciled into workable consensus approaches to issues.
- Through constituency work, members can test such approaches against the practical realities of Canadians' lives. Constituents in turn have in the member an ombudsman, advocate, and source of information on issues of the day.
- As a member of one or more committees of the House, the MP has both the duration of focus to understand issues in some depth and the official standing to comment on them for the public record. Through this avenue, important issues can be brought to the attention of government, the public can be educated and support created for various policy approaches, and potentially vital legislative change can be initiated.
- The House of Commons is where agreements made within party caucuses and in committees are ratified and given concrete legal expression. While often seen as mere formality, our system still requires that legislative action be supported by the specific consent of the majority of members. This means that individual members can seek to delay or prevent actions they disagree with, serving as a check on the arbitrary use of state power. This means that governments can be held to account for their actions and decisions.
- Many members are responsible for a policy portfolio, either as a minister of the Crown or as an opposition critic. Having individual MPs focus on particular policy areas gives parties a knowledgeable, consistent voice on issues and increases public understanding of them. Informed critics promote more thorough public debate, leading, at least in theory, to better public policy.
- MPs also have responsibilities related to maintaining the health of the political parties to which they belong. Healthy political parties is in turn a prerequisite for healthy democratic institutions.

In short, the job of MPs is complex and challenging, and much of it is significant to the health of public institutions and the nation. Our system depends at several key points on the contribution of and vigilance by those who hold elected office. Members of Parliament combine personal, regional and national perspectives. They embody both the co-operation and the competition that make the system work. They defend both individual and collective rights and freedoms. They balance state and individual responsibility.

Canadians depend on the vigilance of Members of Parliament, individually and as a group, to protect the parliamentary system and preserve against the arbitrary use of government power. Ours is a stable system of government precisely because of its ability to reconcile conflicting or competing points of view and bring them into functional harmony. Our capacity to do this as a country is largely responsible for Canada's prosperity and quality of life.

For More Information

Organizations

The Canadian Study of Parliament Group holds regular seminars and publishes their proceedings. The address is Box 660, West Block, Ottawa, Ontario K1A 0A6, telephone (613) 996-0707; fax (613) 992-3674.

Monographs

Dawson, R.M., and W.F. Dawson. *Democratic Government in Canada.* Fifth edition. Toronto: University of Toronto Press, 1989.

Fox, Paul W., and Graham White. *Politics: Canada.* Seventh edition. Toronto: McGraw-Hill Ryerson Ltd., 1991.

Franks, C.E.S. *The Parliament of Canada.* Toronto: University of Toronto Press, 1987.

Jackson, R.J., and D. Jackson. *Politics in Canada: Culture, Institutions, Behaviour and Public Policy.* Fourth edition. Scarborough: Prentice Hall, 1998.

Mallory, J.R. *The Structure of Canadian Government.* Toronto: Macmillan, 1971.

Schultz, Richard, Orest M. Kruhlak and John C. Terry, ed. *The Canadian Political Process.* Third edition. Toronto: Holt, Rinehart and Winston Canada Limited, 1979.

Sobeco Ernst & Young, *Parliamentarians' Compensation: Report Submitted to the President of the Treasury Board.* Ottawa: 1994.

Van Loon, R.J., and M.S. Whittington. *The Canadian Political System, Environment, Structure & Process.* Toronto: McGraw-Hill, 1971.

Web Sites

The official home page for the Parliament of Canada is at
www.parl.gc.ca.

CPAC online provides information about the parliamentary channel and other
resources at www.cpac.ca.

Hansard on-line is accessible from the Parliament of Canada web site.

The Value of Members' Compensation Over Time and Compared with that of Other Occupations

RESEARCH PAPER 5

Research Paper 5

This paper consists of two tables showing the value of members' compensation over time and comparing it with average salaries in other occupations.

Table 1 shows the evolution of the sessional indemnity of Members of Parliament since 1867, with the amount converted to 1996 dollars in the last column of the table.

Table 2 compares members' sessional indemnity with average salaries in other occupations for four different years. The third column of the table shows MPs' salary as a percentage of the average salary for the other occupations, displayed in the second column.

Table 1
Change in the Value of the Sessional Indemnity

Year	Amount of Sessional Indemnity	GWI[1]	CPI Linked to GWI[2]	Sessional Indemnity Converted to 1996 Dollars[3]
1867	$ 600	80.2	8.6	$ 9,416.87
1868	$ 600	80.0	8.6	$ 9,440.41
1869	$ 600	80.7	8.7	$ 9,358.53
1870	$ 600	79.8	8.6	$ 9,464.07
1871	$ 600	81.3	8.6	$ 9,289.46
1872	$ 600	90.6	9.8	$ 9,335.91
1873[4]	**$1,000**	**90.9**	**9.8**	**$13,847.32**
1874	$1,000	86.4	9.3	$14,568.54
1875	$1,000	82.8	8.9	$15,201.95
1876	$1,000	77.6	8.4	$16,220.64
1877	$1,000	73.4	7.9	$17,148.80
1878	$1,000	68.0	7.3	$18,510.61
1879	$1,000	65.5	7.1	$19,217.13
1880	$1,000	71.8	7.7	$17,530.94
1881	$1,000	72.4	7.8	$17,385.66
1882	$1,000	72.5	7.8	$17,361.68
1883	$1,000	70.2	7.6	$17,930.51
1884	$1,000	67.0	7.2	$18,786.89
1885	$1,000	63.3	6.8	$19,885.02
1886	$1,000	62.3	6.7	$20,204.20
1887	$1,000	63.7	6.9	$19,760.15
1888	$1,000	66.2	7.1	$19,013.92
1889	$1,000	66.1	7.1	$19,042.69
1890	$1,000	67.1	7.2	$18,758.89
1891	$1,000	67.1	7.2	$18,758.89
1892	$1,000	62.3	6.7	$20,204.20
1893	$1,000	63.2	6.8	$19,916.48
1894	$1,000	59.1	6.4	$21,298.17
1895	$1,000	57.9	6.2	$21,739.58
1896	$1,000	55.9	6.0	$22,517.38
1897	$1,000	56.8	6.1	$22,160.59
1898	$1,000	59.4	6.4	$21,190.60
1899	$1,000	60.6	6.5	$20,770.99

1   General Wholesale Index, excluding gold. Figures for this index are used only until 1914, when the Consumer Price Index began to be used instead.
2   Consumer Price Index linked to General Wholesale Index excluding gold. Figures for CPI before 1914 are estimates.
3   Conversion factors provided by the Bank of Canada in October 1997.
4   Bold type indicates a year in which the indemnity was changed.

Year	Amount of Sessional Indemnity	GWI[1]	CPI Linked to GWI[2]	Sessional Indemnity Converted to 1996 Dollars[3]
1900	$1,000	62.4	6.7	$20,171.82
1901	**$1,500**	**63.7**	**6.9**	**$29,640.23**
1902	$1,500	66.6	7.2	$28,349.59
1903	$1,500	67.5	7.3	$27,971.59
1904	$1,500	68.3	7.4	$27,643.96
1905	**$2,500**	**70.4**	**7.6**	**$44,698.93**
1906	$2,500	70.7	7.6	$44,509.26
1907	$2,500	76.4	8.2	$41,188.54
1908	$2,500	76.3	8.2	$41,242.52
1909	$2,500	77.6	8.4	$40,551.60
1910	$2,500	78.5	8.5	$40,086.68
1911	$2,500	81.1	8.7	$38,801.53
1912	$2,500	85.2	9.2	$36,934.32
1913	$2,500	83.4	9.0	$37,731.47
1914	$2,500	85.4	9.2	$36,847.83
1915	$2,500		9.4	$36,063.83
1916	$2,500		10.2	$33,235.29
1917	$2,500		12.0	$28,250.00
1918	$2,500		13.6	$24,926.47
1919	$2,500		14.9	$22,751.68
1920	**$4,000**		**17.3**	**$31,352.60**
1921	$4,000		15.2	$35,684.21
1922	$4,000		14.0	$38,742.86
1923	$4,000		14.0	$38,742.86
1924	$4,000		13.7	$39,591.24
1925	$4,000		13.9	$39,021.58
1926	$4,000		14.0	$38,742.86
1927	$4,000		13.8	$39,304.35
1928	$4,000		13.8	$39,304.35
1929	$4,000		14.0	$38,742.86
1930	$4,000		13.9	$39,021.58
1931	$4,000		12.6	$43,047.62
1932	$4,000		11.4	$47,578.95
1933	$4,000		10.9	$49,761.47
1934	$4,000		11.0	$49,309.09
1935	$4,000		11.1	$48,864.86
1936	$4,000		11.3	$48,000.00
1937	$4,000		11.7	$46,358.97
1938	$4,000		12.2	$44,966.10
1939	$4,000		12.9	$46,358.97
1940	$4,000		13.5	$44,459.02
1941	$4,000		13.7	$42,046.51

Year	Amount of Sessional Indemnity	GWI[1]	CPI Linked to GWI[2]	Sessional Indemnity Converted to 1996 Dollars[3]
1942	$ 4,000		13.8	$40,177.78
1943	$ 4,000		13.9	$39,591.24
1944	$ 4,000		14.3	$39,304.35
1945	$ 4,000		15.7	$39,021.58
1946	$ 4,000		17.9	$37,930.07
1947	$ 4,000		18.5	$34,547.77
1948	$ 4,000		19.0	$30,301.68
1949	$ 4,000		21.1	$29,318.92
1950	$ 4,000		21.6	$28,547.37
1951	$ 4,000		21.4	$25,706.16
1952	$ 4,000		21.5	$25,111.11
1953	**$ 8,000**		**21.4**	**$50,691.59**
1954	$ 8,000		21.5	$50,455.81
1955	$ 8,000		21.5	$50,455.81
1956	$ 8,000		21.8	$49,761.47
1957	$ 8,000		22.5	$48,213.33
1958	$ 8,000		23.1	$48,961.04
1959	$ 8,000		23.4	$46,358.97
1960	$ 8,000		23.7	$45,772.15
1961	$ 8,000		23.9	$45,389.12
1962	$ 8,000		24.2	$44,826.45
1963	**$12,000**		**24.6**	**$66,146.34**
1964	$12,000		25.1	$64,828.69
1965	$12,000		25.7	$63,315.18
1966	$12,000		26.6	$61,172.93
1967	$12,000		27.6	$58,956.52
1968	$12,000		28.7	$56,696.86
1969	$12,000		30.0	$54,240.00
1970	$12,000		31.0	$52,490.32
1971	**$18,000**		**31.9**	**$76,514.11**
1972	$18,000		33.4	$73,077.84
1973	$18,000		36.0	$67,800.00
1974	**$24,000**		**39.9**	**$81,563.91**
1975	$24,400		44.2	$73,628.96
1976	$24,400		47.5	$68,513.68
1977	**$25,500**		**51.3**	**$67,403.51**
1978	**$26,900**		**55.9**	**$65,252.95**
1979	**$28,600**		**61.0**	**$63,576.39**
1980	**$40,200**		**67.2**	**$81,117.86**
1981	$43,800		75.5	$78,665.96
1982	$48,600		83.7	$78,735.48
1983	$50,300		88.5	$77,069.83

Year	Amount of Sessional Indemnity	GWI[1]	CPI Linked to GWI[2]	Sessional Indemnity Converted to 1996 Dollars[3]
1984	$52,800		92.4	$77,485.71
1985	$54,600		96.0	$77,122.50
1986	$56,100		100.0	$76,071.60
1987	$57,400		104.4	$74,554.02
1988	$58,300		108.6	$72,794.48
1989	$60,000		114.0	$71,368.42
1990	$62,100		119.5	$70,466.61
1991	$64,400		126.2	$69,196.83
1992	$64,400		128.1	$68,170.49
1993	$64,400		130.4	$66,968.10
1994	$64,400		130.7	$66,814.38
1995	$64,400		133.5	$65,413.03
1996	$64,400		135.6	$64,400.00
1997	$64,400			

Source: Statistics Canada, Prices Division, special tabulation for the Commission.

Table 2
Sessional Indemnity of Members of Parliament
Compared with Average Salaries in Other Occupations

Occupation	Average Salary 1980	MPs' Salary as a percentage
Dentist	$56,874	71.0
Physician/Surgeon	$56,539	71.0
Member of Parliament	**$40,200**	
Lawyer/Notary	$39,030	103.0
Administrator/School	$33,365	120.0
Commissioned Officer	$26,756	150.0
High School Teacher	$25,361	159.0
Accountant	$24,814	162.0
Pharmacist	$24,694	163.0

Occupation	Average Salary 1985	MPs' Salary as a percentage
Physician/Surgeon	$85,023	64.0
Dentist	$75,792	72.0
Lawyer/Notary	$56,430	97.0
Member of Parliament	**$54,600**	
Administrator/School	$45,181	121.0
Commissioned Officer	$39,498	138.0
High School Teacher	$36,245	151.0
Pharmacist	$35,861	152.0
Accountant	$34,043	160.0

Occupation	Average Salary 1990	MPs' Salary as a percentage
Physician/Surgeon	$102,370	61.0
Dentist	$ 95,776	65.0
Lawyer/Notary	$ 78,966	81.0
Member of Parliament	**$ 62,100**	
Administrator/School	$ 54,881	113.0
Commissioned Officer	$ 47,898	130.0
Pharmacist	$ 47,024	132.0
High School Teacher	$ 44,970	138.0
Accountant	$ 42,307	147.0

Occupation	Average Salary 1996	MPs' Salary as a percentage
Physician/Surgeon	$129,036	50.0
Dentist	$106,661	60.0
Lawyer/Notary	$ 95,213	68.0
Secondary School Principal	$ 86,346	75.0
Pharmacist	$ 72,714	89.0
Accountant	$ 66,198	97.0
Army Major	$ 65,362	99.0
Member of Parliament	**$ 64,400**	
Average Teacher	$ 56,000	115.0

Source: Statistics Canada.

The Effects of Service as an MP
on Members' Financial Situation

RESEARCH
PAPER 6

CONTENTS

Research Paper 6

The Effects of Service as an MP on Members' Financial Situation

A fair and reasonable consideration of the remuneration of Members of Parliament must include a look at how their personal financial situation is affected by service in the House of Commons.

While there is little in the way of hard data, for reasons explained later in this paper, it is possible to identify issues, clarify some cases, and provide suggestions for further research, with the aim of giving the discussion of income additional context and perspective.

A relevant place to begin is with the understanding that this is not a lifetime career; most MPs serve for only a short period, returning to the career they left when they were elected, or finding another line of work. This pattern suggested the three focus areas of this paper — MPs' pre-parliamentary careers and financial situation, the situation while they hold office, and the post-parliamentary situation.

What stage of life have MPs reached when first elected? The first section looks at the kind of life members come from and the kind of change election brings. The second focus area is the term of office: do MPs find the income they receive sufficient to cover all their expenses, and does it allow them to accumulate assets as others at a similar stage of life and in comparable occupations are able to do? The third consideration is whether service as an MP adds to their capacity to earn income in the future, after their parliamentary term is over.

Achieving a full understanding of these questions is hampered by several obstacles. Personal finances are a private matter that few Canadians are willing to discuss for public attribution, and MPs are no different. Longitudinal research that assured anonymity by examining the situation of many MPs over several parliaments might help overcome this obstacle, but even if such research were considered useful, a commission such as this does not have the resources to carry it out and also faces a statutory deadline that virtually precludes long-term studies of this type.

Yet even at a general level, without the benefit of extensive data, the issues remain important in discussions of the remuneration of Members of Parliament and should be considered by a commission reviewing the financial arrangements for members. The approach used in this paper involves the best alternative sources of information: a review of the political science literature, a review of the published work of previous review commissions, discussion off the record with elected members, and discussions with experts in employment placement and remuneration to place the experience of MPs in context with that of other Canadians at a similar stage of life.

Despite the difficulties of reaching definitive answers, the subject is well worth considering. As an earlier commission to review allowances of Members of Parliament put it,

> The best from all walks of life are needed to govern Canada. As Canadians, therefore, we ought to do what is reasonably possible to encourage those most qualified to become Members of Parliament and to continue serving this country.[1]

Income Before Election

What financial situation do new members come from? One commission, the 1979 Hales commission, studied the background of those then serving in the House of Commons and found that most Members of Parliament were neither unusually poor nor unusually wealthy before their election victory. Rather, they were much like average members of the middle class and came mostly from one of three lines of work — the law, teaching or administration. This pattern seems to have continued since then.

There have been exceptions, however. The Progressive Conservative sweep of 1984, the defeat of all but two of those new members two elections later, and the substantial cohort of Bloc Québécois members and Reform members from the west brought many people to the Hill who had little previous political experience. In a sweep, many of the members elected tend not to be well established politically before their election. In the absence of a sweep, some of these members would have little chance of election; many would agree to stand as candidates simply to ensure that their party was represented on the ballot. Not all such candidates would have established careers or significant assets; in fact, some might have held relatively junior positions and earned modest incomes.

Notwithstanding the sweep phenomenon, in a relatively stable political system like Canada's, most candidates of a party considered likely to win would have to be in early middle career. They would need to be well-enough known in community or party circles to be able to secure a nomination and respected enough to be considered likely to attract voters who did not yet know them.

What would their income be? In 'winnable' constituencies, potential candidates would have to be considered well established and reasonably successful in a career to attract the support of the nominating committee, so their incomes would likely be at least average for their profession and age. Many lawyers, teachers and administrators in this situation, for example, would be earning roughly what a member of the House of Commons earns. In addition, as a desirable characteristic for candidates is visibility in the community, candidates are likely to have had a history of community involvement and contribution to various causes — activities that seldom produce additional income or leave time for extra career and other income-producing activities. As a result, people with this background who seek election would be unlikely to have accumulated anything more in the way of personal assets than the average middle-class person.

---

1   *Commission to Review Allowances of Members of Parliament* (St. Germain-Fox commission), (Ottawa: 1989), p. xix.

Do candidates seek election for the money? The March 1994 Angus Reid survey of 1500 respondents across Canada, commissioned by the Lapointe commission, showed that these considerations were not well understood by the public. People thought Members of Parliament spent between 40 and 49 hours a week at work and that their income was considerably higher than was in fact the case. Given that respondents whose own income was lower were most likely to underestimate the workload and overestimate the income of MPs, it is possible that some people who win nominations have unrealistic expectations, but it is unlikely that most candidates do, for the facts about salary and benefits are easy to discover.

In the absence of hard data, the conclusion would seem to be that, with some exceptions, most people elected to Parliament earned about the same as what they come to earn as members and do not seek election as a means of improving their incomes.

Income During Service

Parliament has reviewed members' remuneration regularly to ensure that it is adequate and reasonable and that MPs can maintain an attitude of independence and autonomy. The sessional indemnity (the term applied to MPs' salary) has been maintained at a level roughly comparable to the salary of a mid-level professional.

The basic remuneration package for members of the House of Commons consists of the sessional indemnity of $64,400, $21,300 as an incidental expense allowance (no receipts needed), and $6,000 for travel and accommodation (receipts needed). Additional amounts are available for those occupying certain positions of responsibility and for the extra costs involved in representing a large or remote constituency.

Studies by several previous review commissions and independent consultants have shown that the total compensation package is within the broad range of private- and public-sector equivalents. Because the sessional indemnity and incidental expense allowance have been frozen since 1991, however, the relative value of the package has declined by comparison with the remuneration received by other professionals in recent years. The seasonal indemnity portion, for example, was comparable to what a lawyer was earning in 1980 (using 1981 census figures), but was only 68 per cent of a lawyer's salary in 1996.[2]

Another factor in assessing adequacy and reasonableness is to determine whether the compensation package gives members a reasonable expectation of doing what other Canadians with comparable backgrounds and occupations and at a similar stage of life can do — pay down debt, make provision for their children's education, save for retirement. Given that most MPs are in what would be their peak earning years in a non-parliamentary career, are they able to live on less than their current income and so build up assets while serving in Parliament?

Members have reported to review commissions over the years that they find the cost of life as a Member of Parliament unexpectedly high, that they tend to use up any existing capital rather than build it up, and that they do not have time to work for supplementary income.

---

2   Research Paper 5, prepared for this Commission, deals with this issue and is reproduced elsewhere in this volume.

A new member arriving in Ottawa discovers, for example, that housing is more expensive than in most parts of the country. Decisions have to be made about maintaining a residence in the constituency, moving the family to Ottawa, or maintaining two residences. No solution is ideal. Leaving the family in the constituency takes its toll on family life, while commuting or maintaining two residences adds accommodation costs and may result in the loss of the family's second income if the spouse has to leave his or her employment to accompany the MP to Ottawa.

Writing in 1989, the St. Germain-Fox commission said,

It is easier for those MPs with grown or no children or those who are independently wealthy. They, however, are in the minority. Most MPs are middle-income earners with families. In this, they are representative of most Canadians.[3]

The cost of establishing a new home and maintaining two households, even for a few years, and the incidental costs of travel to the constituency most weekends are higher than most people expect. There is general agreement that the housing allowance of $6,000 — or $500 a month — is not enough to cover the cost of basic accommodation in Ottawa.

The St. Germain-Fox commission found that

Most MPs use 100 per cent of their expense allowance on legitimate costs directly related to their work as representatives of their constituency. Many spend more than their allowance and must dip into their own pockets.[4]

By contrast, most business people working for large corporations are reimbursed the full cost of expenses while travelling, including accommodation, food and other costs. Often there is no upper limit on the amount that can be spent in a year, unlike the situation for MPs, whose expense allowance is limited, regardless of actual costs. For business people whose travel expenses are not reimbursed, such as independent sales people, these costs can be deducted from income before income tax is calculated.

The McIsaac-Balcer commission heard from several members on this issue. A typical comment was as follows:

Unless you are willing to divorce your family, a family man should not become a Member of Parliament. Families suffer emotionally, sociologically and economically. Even with subsidy from personal equity, which is rapidly depleting, my family lives at a lower standard than we did before I came to Ottawa, and my net worth is 30% lower. I will not divorce my family and therefore I will probably not run again and instead return to the community and rebuild my equity. Parliament is structured for the very young, the very old and independently wealthy people.[5]

---

3   St. Germain-Fox commission, p. xviii.
4   St. Germain-Fox commission, p. 22.
5   *Commission to Review Allowances of Members of Parliament* (McIsaac-Balcer commission), (Ottawa: 1980), p. 5.

In short, the unsettled life, the extensive and sometimes unexpected social demands, and the personal cost of elections do not create conditions in which it is easy for any but the most frugal members to save from their income, especially since, according to a study by Hay Management Consultants Limited for the St. Germain-Fox commission, Members of Parliament received about 20 per cent less compensation than comparable workers in other sectors.

How many MPs can or do supplement their income with other work? All the review commissions to date have agreed that the job of MP is a full-time one and has been since at least the 1970s.

The Clarke-Campbell commission said in their 1984 report:

Clearly, the Member of Parliament today has a demanding, full-time occupation. Yet more than half of those responding to our questionnaire said they find it necessary to supplement their parliamentary income to live in their usual manner. By 1984 less than one-fifth said they worked outside of Parliament. The day of the part-time MP is over.[6]

Some members of the public believe that MPs are overpaid or that in any case the benefits of being a member outweigh the costs:

...opponents of parliamentary pay increases often argue that public life brings with it a certain amount of offsetting 'psychic income', that is, the prestige and trappings of power.... The Commission notes that, in the eyes of many MPs such 'psychic income' is already balanced by what may be called the 'psychic costs' of public life. These psychic costs, unique to parliamentary life, can include

- the stress and estrangement placed on families and domestic relations;
- the fatigue and strain of travel and 60-hour-plus weeks;
- the tension and anxiety which can come from the legislator's uncertain tenure of office and from the interruption of the development of private-sector job skills and security required by public service; and
- the frequent loss of privacy and public criticism which is incurred by a public figure in a democratic society.[7]

How many MPs are able to maintain their previous income while working full-time as a member? The increasing demands of the work since 1984 mean that likely even fewer MPs — especially not those representing constituencies outside the National Capital Region — are able to work at a second job. It might be possible for an MP to keep a business open with family help or hired management. In fact, however, most report that they are too busy to work part-time or to manage assets.

Furthermore, most members are not in a position to maintain previous employment and income during a term of parliamentary service. Fields such as teaching and management do not lend themselves easily to working part-time or maintaining previous income levels. Similarly, lawyers find that if they do not consistently bring in new clients, their position in a firm becomes untenable. In short, given the cost of

---

6   *Commission to Review Allowances of Members of Parliament* (Clarke-Campbell commission), (Ottawa: 1985), p. 6.

7   Clarke-Campbell commission, p. xxvii.

life as an MP and the limited opportunities to supplement income through additional employment, it is unlikely that any member returns to private life after an average stay in Parliament with more equity than they had before they were elected.

Options After Parliament

The typical MP does not stay in Parliament for long. Relatively few are in the House for even a decade. Some quit because they no longer wish to put up with the frustrations and personal sacrifices. Most, however, lose their seats at election time.[8]

A previous review commission studied the longevity of parliamentarians and found that "The average mean period for which a person is a Member of the House of Commons is 4.6 years."[9]

C.E.S. Franks sums it up this way in his book, *The Parliament of Canada:*
a high proportion of Canadian MPs are learning their job, and a equally large proportion are planning to leave, expecting to leave, going to leave, or all three.[10]

Whether because of defeat or retirement, at some time most members will find themselves looking for new work, sometimes unexpectedly. The average MP is about 50 (the average in the 35th Parliament was 51.5 years, in the 36th Parliament, 49.3 years). An actuarial report prepared for the Office of the Superintendent of Financial Institutions showed that a 50-year-old MP has a 42-per cent chance of losing his or her job during an election year.[11] This probability is higher for MPs elected most recently. What happens to them when they have to leave, as most do after one or two terms? Does their income increase or decrease at that time?

The answer depends on several factors. As discussed earlier, a few members have work that can be resumed after leaving Parliament, but this is far from being the rule. Outplacement agencies indicate that being about 50 is not necessarily an impediment to finding new work and that qualified people of that age will likely land on their feet eventually. The question is, how soon?

Like anyone suddenly or unexpectedly out of work, MPs need a transition period. The average defeated member would have spent about five years on the Hill focusing intensely on matters that might or might not translate into workplace skills or be of interest to a prospective employer. The former MP might be exhausted from the election campaign or even depressed in the face of an unanticipated defeat. The speed with which they deal with the new situation will depend on how quickly they are able to organize themselves to present their experience in a form that employers can understand and how flexible they are in adapting to a non-parliamentary workplace and learning new skills where needed. They will also need to learn current job-search methods, including, for example, use of the Internet.

---

8   Paul Fox and Graham White, *Politics: Canada* (Toronto: McGraw-Hill, 1991), p. 410.
9   St. Germain-Fox commission, p. 41.
10   C.E.S. Franks, *The Parliament of Canada* (Toronto: University of Toronto Press, 1987), p. 75.
11   "The Actuarial Report as at 31 March 1995", Pension Plan for Members of Parliament (Ottawa: Office of the Superintendent of Financial Institutions, 1996).

According to research by Murray Axsmith & Associates, most people in the MPs' salary range take about six months to find work. However, their research also shows that age discrimination does exist. "There are well-documented cases of real difficulties. Our statistics show that the person over 55 takes an average of two months longer to complete a job search."[12]

Circumstances can vary for those in different parties and at different times. A defeated government member whose party remains in power, for example, may be able to retain contacts and access. Ministers are prevented by conflict of interest guidelines from accepting government contracts in their area for two years, but former MPs who are lawyers may find that contacts and government experience make them attractive to law firms. However, not everyone will have useful contacts or be working in a field that would make such contacts useful. It is doubtful that having served with the party in government would help the work prospects of a teacher or administrator, for example.

Members facing a job search after their party loses power and those belonging to one of the smaller parties are unlikely to find that their parliamentary service opens doors for them. As former Progressive Conservative minister John Crosbie put it in his comments at a panel discussion sponsored by the Commission:

> Once you are defeated...you are unsung, unhonoured , unknown and you're unwept. In fact, you might as well be a junkyard dog as far as anybody giving you a hand.

Circumstances are often different for members of different parties defeated in the same election. We saw anecdotal evidence, for example, that some Progressive Conservatives defeated in the 1993 sweep that removed the party from power have found the job search very difficult.

The age of defeated MPs, their work experience, and the circumstances surrounding the election at which they were defeated all make it difficult to generalize about the likely fate of defeated MPs. With an average age of 50, however, what does seem likely is that defeated MPs will use up any separation allowance during a period of post-parliamentary unemployment, even if their job search is eventually successful.

Once they find work, is their income likely to be higher than it would have been in the absence of service in Parliament? MPs returning to their former profession or occupation may find that they have lost touch with the necessary knowledge, skills or practices and need time to catch up. Meanwhile, competitors may have taken advantage of their absence to establish their own positions in the marketplace, or other professionals who were previously junior to the former MP will now have as much or more experience and seniority.

To illustrate the situation facing defeated members, the St. Germain-Fox commission quoted a former member's comments in the House in 1981:

> My four N.D.P. colleagues who went down to defeat in 1980 were not so lucky.... Of the four, not one had a job to go back to the day after the election. One, though, after some months, was reluctantly taken back by his school board

---

12   Murray Axsmith (Ottawa) Limited, personal communication with Rob Notman, president.

because the contract demanded it. Two others still cannot find jobs equal to those they left on first becoming elected, and the third started his own business and is in debt to the bank for thousands of dollars.[13]

Although time did not permit a detailed review of the situation following more recent elections, there is ample anecdotal evidence to show that the observations made in 1981 remain valid today.

Having spent time in the public eye is not necessarily an advantage in seeking employment. Serving in Parliament may give some members an opportunity to make their personality and abilities well known, but by the same token, errors and missteps also become public knowledge. Moreover, the skills involved in establishing a public profile are not necessarily desirable in or transferrable to the private sector, nor does their presence always indicate policy or administrative skills. Some MPs remain relatively unknown despite obvious talent and energy, and for them parliamentary service clearly provides no subsequent advantage.

Service in Parliament may carry some advantage for members who return to or take up certain professions after election defeat. Legal firms, communications firms, and government relations and other consulting firms have been known to employ former members. Those who were members of the government party, for example, may benefit from contacts and access if the party is still in power, although their activities in this regard are somewhat circumscribed by conflict of interest guidelines.

Parliament does provide a pension for defeated and retired members with at least six years' service, available at age 55. The St. Germain-Fox commission found that

> After having reviewed all sides of the issue, the Commissioners believe that the current pension benefits are adequate at the present time.[14]

The Sobeco study on parliamentarians' compensation, prepared for the Treasury Board in 1994, found that this pension was at least as generous as that available to most professionals and that the overall compensation package was comparable to those of occupations they considered equivalent (that is, the income portion might be lower for MPs but the pension was higher).[15] Based on this study, the Lapointe commission found that the retirement allowance for MPs was essentially equal to that for people doing comparable work elsewhere.

The pension does provide for much faster accrual than the average pension plan, in a way similar to the plans of corporate chief executive officers and others in high-risk jobs. However, this pension is not portable to most situations in the private sector.

Most MPs do not have additional room to contribute to an RRSP while also contributing to the MPs' pension plan. Those with more than six years' service get no severance pay to cover a period of career transition, and pension benefits are not available until age 55. An MP with sufficient means to cover the transition period can deposit the severance sum in an RRSP (and the amount is equivalent to the employer's contribution to a pension in any case), but those without such means will likely have to spend their severance payment — in effect, negating any retirement benefit, and they must pay tax on the capital as well.

---

13 House of Commons, *Debates,* 9 July 1981, p. 11,383.
14 St. Germain-Fox commission, p. 42.
15 Sobeco, Ernst & Young, *Parliamentarians' Compensation,* Report Submitted to the President of the Treasury Board (1994).

The pension is larger than that available to legislators in some other countries, and options for changing it in various ways have been discussed. The Sobeco report commented, for example,

> An interesting factor in France and Sweden is that the Parliamentarian's personal financial situation upon his or her return to private life has an impact on the amounts he or she is entitled to receive.[16]

Not all retiring MPs are eligible for a pension, however. As the St. Germain-Fox commission pointed out,

> In 1988, there were 113 Members who did not return to the House of Commons. They either retired or were defeated in the election. Of these 113 former Members, 51 received pensions and 62 did not. Put another way, after the 1988 election, the majority (55 per cent) of former Members of the House of Commons did not receive a pension.[17]

Further Research

Many questions could be answered by a prospective study following a cohort of parliamentarians through their working life. Who runs for nomination, and who is chosen? At this stage the study would identify the financial and other characteristics of nominees and find a group of people who are roughly similar to act as a comparison group. How do the characteristics of those who are nominated compare with those who are elected? What happens during their time in Parliament? Do they accumulate assets or spend them? Finally, what happens later? Do financial considerations influence a voluntary decision to leave Parliament? What is their situation immediately after leaving and five and ten years later? The situation of the comparison group would also be examined at each stage.

Such a project would supply hard data that is currently missing. The difficulty would lie in getting agreement from the subjects to disclose their financial situation over a 20-year period and maintaining contact with those no longer in public life.

A less demanding study could be done with former parliamentarians. The study would involve asking a random sample about their experiences, using a questionnaire or other formal means of gathering information. Personal reflections and recollections are not always accurate, but the data could be useful. Maintaining anonymity and gaining co-operation could be obstacles. To help with this, the association of former parliamentarians might be prepared to choose the sample and handle mailing.

A third possible study would involve research with riding associations to determine whether qualified candidates were refusing offers made by search committees because of financial and related concerns. Such a study might serve to validate a concern raised by the St. Germain-Fox commission in 1989:

> ...while many dedicated people of quality and talent continue to seek careers in Parliament, the level of parliamentary remuneration and the costs of holding

---

16   Sobeco report, p. 33.
17   St. Germain-Fox commission, p. 41.

public office have combined to prevent many individuals of calibre and public-spiritedness from embarking upon parliamentary careers. Indeed, it has deterred some of those who have recently held office from seeking it again.[18]

Finally, it would be valuable to know the extent of the understanding new members have of the likely financial demands on them and how well equipped they are to deal with it. According to the executive search company Drake Beam Morin, it is common practice in the private sector to provide information for new employees to help them adjust to their new position and to prepare them to work effectively in the new circumstances. Parliament does have a program to orient new members. Is it adequate and appropriate for all new members? For example, do new MPs have a clear understanding of the financial demands on them? Do they have the personal knowledge and resources necessary to plan for themselves and their families in a realistic way? If not, what type of program would be helpful, and how could it be delivered in a manner acceptable to those it was intended to assist? Could such a program be implemented at a reasonable cost, for example, by including sessions on personal finances and career planning in existing orientation programs? Or would an individual approach be more appropriate?

Conclusion

The purpose of this paper was to present an understanding of where parliamentarians come from professionally and financially, how they fare financially during their elected term, and their options afterward. The general conclusion is that the effect of service on the typical MP's lifetime financial situation is probably neutral overall, but it is impossible to ignore the often significant disruption that service in Parliament represents for many members.

Before being elected, most future MPs are working in one of three professions — teaching, management/administration, or the law. Given the average age at election, most are at what would be the mid-point of their career, earning at least the average for their age and profession. This level of income is generally similar to that of an MP. With some exceptions, then, the transition from private life to elected life represents neither a windfall nor a major financial loss for most MPs.

Once in office, the situation may change for some members. The life of a parliamentarian is unsettled and demanding, with constant travel and, for some, the need to maintain two households, creating additional expenses. With a family income roughly similar to what they had before election (or even lower, if the spouse has given up a job to move to Ottawa), accumulating savings might be difficult. Moreover, given the nature of their previous careers and the time demands of parliamentary life, few MPs are likely to be able to supplement their incomes through involvement in a business or part-time work in a previous occupation. At the end of a term in the House of Commons, then, an MP is unlikely to be better off financially than before election. Some may actually be worse off relative to their peers; they may not have been able to accumulate savings as they would have if they had remained in their previous career, or they may have had to dip into savings for expenses not covered by their parliamentary income.

---

18   St. Germain-Fox commission, p. xxv.

Some consider that other aspects of the job — its ostensible glamour and prestige, for example — are adequate compensation. In fact, however, the patina of these apparent perquisites tarnishes quickly. The first plane trip may be fun, but the hundredth is more likely to be gruelling, especially when it is part of a 70-hour work week and means separation from home and family.

After parliamentary service, a great deal depends on the circumstances, health and energy of the individual. Not everyone is ready to start over at 50, the average age at which a parliamentary career ends. Most people at that age find a job search takes several months at least, and the circumstances prompting the search are not always propitious. Many former MPs will be experiencing the stress of job loss and, being older, may be less able or inclined to resume aggressive career-building.

After an average of four or five years away from a profession or career, former members may find that they have lost ground relative to their peers. Colleagues have moved up the ladder in terms of income and career progression. Younger people have entered the profession. Former members' knowledge and skills may have been eroded, and they have no recent experience in the field. Business people, entrepreneurs and independent professionals find that competitors have been busy in their absence. The result may be a lower earning potential than they would have had if they had remained in the previous career. In addition, retiring or defeated MPs may have less capital than they would otherwise have had.

A pension that accumulates quickly compensates for this to a certain extent, but studies of the pension plan have not found the pension to be out of proportion. The special case is defeated members who are not eligible for a pension and not able to find work before their separation allowance runs out. An assessment of how to close this gap in financial arrangements is worth considering. Although members should not expect special financial advantages as a result of service in Parliament, it is reasonable that service to the country should not leave them appreciably worse off than they were before being elected.

For More Information

Publications

Commission to Review Allowances of Members of Parliament (St. Germain-Fox commission), (Ottawa: 1989).

Commission to Review Allowances of Members of Parliament (Lapointe commission), *Democratic Ideals and Financial Realities: Paying Representatives in the 21st Century* (Ottawa: 1994).

Sobeco, Ernst & Young, *Parliamentarians' Compensation*, Report Submitted to the President of the Treasury Board (1994).

Paul Fox and Graham White, *Politics: Canada* (Toronto: McGraw-Hill, 1991).

C.E.S. Franks, *The Parliament of Canada* (Toronto: University of Toronto Press, 1987).

Office of the Superintendent of Financial Institutions, "Actuarial Report as at 31 March 1995", Pension Plan for Members of Parliament (Ottawa: 1996).

Organizations

The Association of Former Parliamentarians is chaired by Barry Turner and can be reached at their office on Parliament Hill.

Murray Axsmith (Ottawa) Ltd., Rob Notman, president (613) 238-6266; notman@murrayaxsmith.com.

Drake Beam Morin (Ottawa) Inc., Suite 1510–360 Albert Street, Ottawa, Ontario (613) 235-0076.

William M. Mercer Ltd., Consulting Actuaries, attention: M. Cohen, 1100–275 Slater Street, Ottawa, Ontario (613) 230-9348.

Review of Pensions and Benefits
for Members of Parliament

RESEARCH
PAPER 7

CONTENTS

Research Paper 7

Review of Pensions and Benefits for Members of Parliament[1]

This report reviews existing arrangements for the pensions and benefits of members of the House of Commons and comments on alternative plan designs that would respond better to their needs. In particular, the report looks at the issue of opting out of the pension plan. It also compares MPs' benefits with those provided by other employers in the public and private sectors. The report also looks briefly at retirement arrangements for members of the Senate.

Main Findings

The main findings of this report are as follows:

- The incidental expense allowance should be grossed-up and added to pensionable salary, with an adjustment to the accrual rate.
- The current defined benefit plan could be retained for those who wish to participate in it, but the accrual rate should be reduced to 2.5 per cent, resulting in the same annual benefit accrual as at present.
- A permanent opting-out feature could be considered, giving current and future MPs the choice of opting out of the current plan.
- Those opting out would become members of an alternative defined contribution pension arrangement.
- The severance allowance should be separated from the pension plan and paid to all members who are not in receipt of an immediate pension on leaving the House of Commons.
- MPs who opted out in the 35th Parliament could be permitted to opt back in to the current plan.
- MPs who continue to opt out of the current plan could not be given any tax-sheltered compensation for past years opted out.
- Senators' sessional indemnity and pension should be treated the same way as MPs'.
- Benefit plans are in line with those with which we compared them, but they have not kept pace with recent trends.
- Benefit plans for members should be reviewed at the same time as those for executives in the public service.

---

1   This paper was prepared for the Commission to Review Allowances of Members of Parliament by William M. Mercer Limited of Ottawa and completed in December 1997.

Background

Salary and Expense Allowance

Members of Parliament are paid a regular taxable salary (the sessional indemnity) and an incidental expense allowance, which is not taxable and for which receipts are not required. The indemnity and allowance are as follows:

	Members of the House of Commons	Members of the Senate
Sessional indemnity	$64,400	$64,400
Incidental expense allowance	$21,300	$10,100

Additional amounts are paid in some cases: for example, members of either house who hold positions of extra responsibility (ministers, party leaders, the speaker) are paid an additional indemnity; members representing large or remote constituencies are paid an additional expense allowance. This report concentrates on a review of pensions and benefits in relation to the basic salary and allowances only.

The Pension Plan

The pension plan for MPs provides for an accrual rate of 4 per cent per year of service to a maximum accrual of 75 per cent after 19 years. The pension is paid on leaving the House of Commons or at age 55, whichever is later. It is indexed to the cost of living; the commencement of indexation is delayed to age 60, at which time adjustments reflecting increases in the Consumer Price Index (CPI) are made retroactively. Members contribute 9 per cent of their sessional indemnity until the maximum benefit has been reached and 1 per cent of the sessional indemnity after that. Contributions and benefits based on the other allowances an MP receives are optional. A summary of plan provisions is provided in Appendix 1.

A minimum of six years' service in the House of Commons is required to qualify for a pension. If the member leaves the House with less than six years' service, a severance allowance of six months' salary is paid in lieu of a pension. No severance allowance is paid once the member qualifies for a pension.

The plan was amended in 1995. Before these amendments, the plan had an accrual rate of 5 per cent per year (to a maximum of 75 per cent after 15 years), payable once the member left the House, regardless of age. Member contributions were also higher, at 11 per cent. Before these changes, membership in the plan was compulsory. The 1995 changes made the plan optional for members in the 35th Parliament. It has again become compulsory for members in the 36th Parliament. This means that new members elected to the current parliament cannot opt out of the plan, but those who opted out in the previous parliament continue not to be members of the plan.

The plan entails an employer cost estimated (by the 1994 Sobeco report) at about 44 per cent of payroll, without taking into account tax considerations (discussed at greater length later in this paper), for the previous 5 per cent per year benefit.[2] We estimate that the 4 per cent per year benefit under the current plan represents an employer cost of just below 35 per cent of payroll. These figures represent an average cost over the whole population: the cost as a percentage of the salary of individual members is quite variable — higher for younger members, who can benefit from the full 19-year accrual, and lower for older members. Also, the average cost over a member's career is lower for those who accumulate the full 75 per cent while still in the House. Further years of service attract no additional benefit, thereby reducing the average cost over the whole career. Appendix 2 shows the approximate cost as a percentage of salary for a number of typical members.

Benefits

We reviewed the benefits program (medical, dental, etc.) and compared it to the broad marketplace, including the public sector (provincial governments, Crown corporations, and 'other' public sector, such as municipalities and school boards) and the private sector. This comparison is particularly relevant given the varied background of MPs.

The MPs' benefit program mirrors benefits provided to executives in the federal public service. Indeed, the core benefits, including the cost-sharing, duplicate those provided at the EX level.

Methodology

Pensions

Our review was based on the analysis in the 1994 Sobeco report. We updated the international and provincial comparisons and noted any important developments in pensions for parliamentarians (or equivalent positions) in the countries or provinces chosen for comparison. We also reviewed the conclusions of the report and comment on and update them in this paper.

In this paper we review the general rationale for providing pension plans and the specific rationale for plans for elected officials, given their rather different career path from that of employees. This leads to a comparison of typical plan designs for different kinds of employees. We also examine briefly some of the public perception issues that might influence the outcome of this analysis. With regard to the issue of public perceptions, we look specifically at the question of the incidental expense allowance and its impact in the case of the pension plan.

Finally, we look at some alternatives to the current pension plan and give some approximate costs of the alternatives, as well as sample pensions for typical members under various plan designs.

Benefits

Ideally, the methodology should be based on the relative value of the total package of benefits for typical members as compared to benefits for employees in other

---

2   Sobeco Ernst & Young, *Parliamentarians' Compensation*, study commissioned by the Treasury Board (Ottawa: 1994). The Sobeco report, released in February 1994, analyzed the terms and conditions of employment for Members of Parliament.

organizations.[3] This report uses a more limited methodology, basically testing members' perception that their benefit package is less generous than that of organizations in which members may have been employed before being elected.

The package is compared generally, in terms of benefits and employee contributions, to the package available to federal public servants and to typical packages in the public and private sectors. An overall judgement about the relative generosity of the plan can then be made.

The analysis includes a brief overview of current trends in employee benefits that may be colouring members' view of the relative generosity of the benefits available to them.

Review of the Sobeco Report
Pensions
International Comparisons

Comparisons were made with six countries: Australia, the United Kingdom, Belgium, Sweden, France, and the United States.

All the plans examined were defined benefit plans with varying benefit levels. In terms of cost, Sobeco's estimate of 44 per cent of payroll (based on the 5 per cent formula) placed the Canadian plan below the cost for Australia and Belgium, but above the cost for the other countries. The 4 per cent formula and minimum age of 55 would reduce the cost of the Canadian plan to less than 35 per cent, placing the Canadian plan on a par with France's (at 34 per cent) but still above the cost of the U.K., Swedish and U.S. plans, all with costs of 15 to 17 per cent of payroll.

None of the countries has changed its plan since the Sobeco report. We obtained additional information about some of the plans, however, that supplements and, in some cases, corrects data in the Sobeco report. These revisions are shown in Appendix 5.

Provincial Comparisons

In the Sobeco comparison, the federal plan was very similar to three provincial plans (Ontario, Quebec and British Columbia), in terms of both benefit formula and overall cost. This is not surprising, as the federal plan tends to be a model for the provinces. Ontario and B.C. had costs that were comparable to the federal cost (46 per cent and 45 per cent respectively), while the cost of the Quebec plan was lower, at 32 per cent, mainly because of the lack of full indexation. The 4 per cent formula would make the federal plan decidedly less expensive than the Ontario and B.C. plans and place it in the same cost range as the Quebec plan. Since the Sobeco report, however, both Ontario and B.C. have eliminated the defined benefit plan that was used for its comparison (see accompanying table, which summarizes the plans that have undergone major changes, as well as the three plans used for the Sobeco comparison).

---

3   In this approach, benefit elements are evaluated using a value approach (the pension plan member's point of view) as opposed to a cost approach (the employer's point of view), considering not only the design of the various benefit elements, but also the actual demographics of the 'typical' employee (based on the demographics of MPs as a group).

Province	Effective date of change	Plan before change	Plan after change
British Columbia	16 June 1996	defined benefit plan	• accruals up to 19 June 1996 payable in accordance with previous plan • no further accruals after 19 June 1996 • authority to set up voluntary RRSP (no details as yet)
Alberta	14 June 1993	defined benefit plan	• members with at least 5 years' service on 14 June 1993 will receive pension under previous plan for service to 14 June 1993 • no plan in place for service after 14 June 1993
Ontario	8 June 1995	defined benefit plan	• accrued benefits to 8 June 1995 payable under terms of previous plan, or converted to defined contribution amount • accrued benefits provided by combination of registered plan and top-up plan • non-contributory defined contribution plan after 8 June 1995 • government contribution of 5% of salary
Quebec	n/a	defined benefit plan	no change: benefit summary as per Sobeco report
P.E.I.	May 1994	defined benefit plan	• member contributions reduced by 2% from 1971 to 1994 • pensions accrued from 1971 to 1994 reduced as of 1994 • indexation reduced to CPI minus 2% • new plan established by independent commission now in place

A more detailed summary of plans for all the provinces is provided in Appendix 4.

Analysis and Recommendations
Pension Plan

The Sobeco report considered it "undesirable" to replace the defined benefit plan with a defined contribution plan. This conclusion is examined further in our analysis of the rationale for pension plans.

The report recommended that pensions not be payable before age 55. This change has been made.

The report recommended that the accrual rate be reduced from 5 per cent to 2 per cent, which is the rate applicable to federal public servants. The rate was reduced to 4 per cent, which is still above that for most plans in the private and public sectors. Again, we return to this issue later in this paper.

The report recommended that the current indexation formula — essentially full CPI indexation that is delayed until age 60 (when retroactive indexation from the date of leaving the House is applied) — be replaced by CPI minus 3 per cent indexation without any delay. No change has been made to the indexation formula. We comment on the issue of indexation later in the paper.

In keeping with the lower accrual rate, the report recommended that the member contribution rate be reduced to 5 per cent. In fact, it was reduced to 9 per cent, which is roughly in line with the reduction of the accrual rate from 5 per cent to 4 per cent.

The report also recommended changes to bring the plan into line with pension regulatory legislation, such as two-year vesting (compared to six years currently) and portability. Neither of these has been implemented.

The report estimated that these changes would reduce the employer cost from 44 per cent of payroll to about 12.5 per cent, although there appears to be an inconsistency between the recommendations and the costing (a minimum age of 55 for the commencement of a pension is recommended, but the costing assumes an earliest retirement age of 60). Also, given current inflation rates, the savings from using a CPI minus 3 per cent formula (but no reduction if inflation is below 3 per cent) may be overestimated.

We estimate that the current employer cost has been reduced to the range of 30 to 35 per cent of payroll (using the Sobeco basis), given the changes actually made.

Benefits

The Sobeco report found the benefits package "attractive" and in line with those for executives in the private sector.

Objectives of Pension Plans and Review of Pension Plans

Retirement Versus Termination

Pension plans are designed generally to provide income from the point at which employees leave the workforce, usually somewhere between the ages of 60 and 65. By contrast, termination benefits are predicated on the employee obtaining further employment between termination and retirement.

In the case of MPs, the period after leaving the House and becoming eligible to collect a parliamentary pension can be very difficult financially relative to the situation of the average employee who resigns or is laid off from a job. In most cases, MPs do not leave the House voluntarily but because they are defeated at the polls. They are therefore in a difficult position, as they may not have prepared themselves for a career change.

MPs with less than six years of service receive a severance allowance equivalent to six months' pay. MPs with more service generally receive a pension, although since the 1995 amendments, this pension does not start until the former member reaches age 55.

It therefore appears that the plan attempted (at least until the 1995 changes) to cover both retirement and career transition, but it may in fact be preferable to treat these issues separately. We return to this later.

Pension Plan Objective and Defined Benefit Versus Defined Contribution Plans

The objective of a pension plan is to provide plan members with sufficient income in retirement to replace most of their pre-retirement income, after taking into account pensions from public sources and income from personal savings and investment. The two main types of pension plan (defined benefit and defined contribution) are both capable of meeting this objective but are subject to different distributions of risks between the employer and plan members and of benefits between types of plan member.

- **Defined benefit.** Under this type of plan, the benefit at retirement is calculated by means of a formula linked to salary and years of membership in the plan. The MPs' plan and the plan for federal public servants (public service superannuation) are defined benefit plans.
- **Defined contribution.** Under this type of plan, employer and employee contributions are fixed in advance, generally as a percentage of salary, and are invested in a fund. At retirement, a pension is purchased, based on annuity rates at the time of purchase. This type of plan encompasses registered defined contribution plans, money purchase plans, and group registered retirement savings plans.

In terms of distribution of benefits between types of members, the following is generally the case.

- Defined benefit plans are more beneficial for older, longer-service employees who retire from the plan and less advantageous for younger, short-service employees who leave the job before retirement.
- Defined contribution plans are more beneficial for short-term younger employees and less beneficial for long-service, older employees.

The accompanying graph illustrates this description by comparing the value of benefits versus accumulated contributions for defined benefit and defined contribution plans.

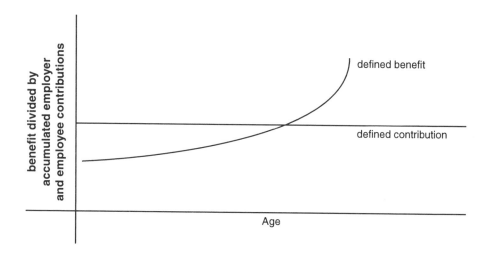

The graph shows that the defined contribution plan is more or less neutral in relation to the age of the plan member, whereas the defined benefit plan rewards older, longer-service employees at the expense of younger, shorter-service members (some of whom, of course, eventually become older, longer-service employees, if they remain with the employer).

The distinction between defined benefit and defined contribution plans is less acute when the deferred pension for employees who leave before retirement is indexed to the CPI. In a non-indexed plan, the contrast between value for early leavers and for retirees is much greater than for indexed plans.

The next table provides an overview of the advantages and disadvantages of the two types of pension plan.

Defined Benefit Plans	
Advantages	**Disadvantages**
• benefit based on fixed formula related to income before retirement • employees insulated from economic and financial risks, especially if plan fully indexed • efficient investment of funds through professional long-term investment	• risks of poor performance allocated to plan sponsor • plan members do not share in superior investment performance • plan members terminating before retirement may lose out (less of a concern in an indexed plan) • less advantageous to short-term employees • less transparency of costs, as this requires actuarial valuation, which depends on a number of actuarial assumptions

Defined Contribution Plans	
Advantages	**Disadvantages**
• employer cost fixed in advance • employee benefits from superior investment performance • generally more advantageous to employees terminating before retirement • greater transparency of costs, as these are stated explicitly, without need for actuarial valuation	• employee bears economic and financial risks • pension as function of pre-retirement income can only be estimated and will fluctuate widely depending on financial conditions • rate of return tends to be lower than in defined benefit plans because of individuals' lack of long-term horizon and retail-level investment

This table shows that both plan types have advantages and disadvantages, whether from the employer's or the members' perspective. In theory, both should be capable of producing the same target benefit at roughly the same cost to employer and employees, although with a different distribution of benefits and risks, provided investment returns are similar for the two types of plan. However, tax implications (discussed in greater detail below) make it difficult in practice to reproduce pensions such as those provided by the MP plan in a defined contribution plan. If the target were more modest, such as those provided under the *Public Service Superannuation Act* (PSSA), then it is possible that the two types of plan could achieve the same target, at least for levels of income represented by the regular sessional indemnity.

Given that more than 90 per cent of pension plan members in Canada and almost all public sector employees belong to defined benefit plans, we concur with the general conclusion of the Sobeco report that it is undesirable to switch to a defined contribution plan design.

Level of Benefits, Vesting, Indexation and Investment

Despite that conclusion, four issues require further attention: the level of benefits in the MP plan, vesting, indexation, and investment of funds.

Level of Benefits

One of the design concepts behind defined benefit plans is the career employee. For example, in the federal public service, employees retiring with 35 years of service receive a benefit equal to 70 per cent of their final average salary, integrated with the Canada Pension Plan (CPP). Together with government benefits, and taking into account tax and other changes during retirement, this level of income will be sufficient to replace most of the employee's pre-retirement income on an after-tax and after-expense basis. In the case of shorter careers, the plan is not as successful at replacing an employee's pre-retirement income.

Members of Parliament are not expected to have quite the same career path as others. They tend to be elected later in life and may serve for only a relatively short period. They may resign or lose an election before a 'normal' retirement age of 60 or 65. Does this justify the design of their current pension plan?

- On one hand, members can be expected to have belonged to a plan or accumulated retirement funds both before and after being in the House, so the plan need only provide the regular accrual for the period in the House.
- On the other hand, members may lose considerable pension entitlement on becoming a Member of Parliament and may not be able to make up for such losses after leaving the House.

To help answer the question, it is instructive to look at the provision of pension benefits to others in positions similar to Members of Parliament.

In the public sector, a PSSA-type plan would be typical. This plan provides a 2 per cent benefit, based on the best six years' average salary, integrated with the CPP. Generous survivor benefits are provided. Employee contributions are 7.5 per cent of salary, less contributions to the CPP. The benefit is fully indexed to the cost of living.

In the private sector, typical unit benefits would be between 1.8 and 2 per cent, integrated with the CPP, if the plan is contributory, and between 1 and 1.3 per cent if non-contributory. Contributions would probably be at a lower level than in public sector plans, typically no more than 5 per cent.

More than 90 per cent of Canada's pension plan members are in defined benefit plans. However, there has been a trend to convert defined benefit plans to defined contribution plans, although this has not had a significant impact on the proportion of members in the two types of plan.

Of particular interest in this context are plans offered executives and chief executive officers (CEOs) hired in mid-career. In the federal public service, deputy ministers who are deputy heads of departments are entitled to 2 per cent per year of service in this position, to a maximum of 10 years, in addition to their PSSA entitlement. This means that after 19 years of service, at least 10 of which were in a deputy minister position, the incumbent would be entitled to a pension of 58 per cent of average salary; after 26 years the pension would be 75 per cent of average salary.

To identify the prevalence and scope of similar plans in the private sector, we looked at data assembled by William M. Mercer Limited on supplementary plans for CEOs. It is likely that other senior executives have similar plans for mid-career hires, but such data are more difficult to extract from our database.

The Mercer survey provides separate data for CEO-specific plans. Data on special plans (i.e., other than plans intended mainly to provide benefits in excess of the *Income Tax Act* maximum) for other senior executives are not readily available from the survey. The results of this survey are shown in Appendix 6.

The DM plan is in addition to the basic PSSA, which provides benefits of 2 per cent per year of service (maximum 35 years), at a contribution rate of 7.5 per cent of salary. Both benefits and contributions are integrated with the CPP.

Likewise, CEO plans generally are in addition to the basic pension plan provided by the organization. Plan designs varied greatly. Some were similar to the DM plan, giving additional benefits per year of service. Others waived the employee contribution that would otherwise be payable. Others merely increased the regular benefit to the *Income Tax Act* maximum accrual amount (2 per cent of three-year indexed final average salary, no CPP integration).

This indicates that the MPs' plan is not necessarily out of line with public and private sector plans that recognize the impact of the mid-career hire aspect of the career path of their senior employees.

One final issue specific to the MPs' plan is the question of salary level. While the sessional indemnity is relatively low, it is supplemented by an incidental expense allowance for which no receipts are necessary and that is not subject to income tax. In effect, at least part of this allowance could be considered salary, in which case it could be grossed up and added to pensionable salary. It is possible that the 4 per cent (previously 5 per cent) accrual rate was intended to take the incidental expense allowance into account. In other words, a 4 per cent accrual rate based on taxable salary is equivalent to about a 2.5 per cent rate based on salary plus grossed-up incidental expense allowance. This issue is discussed at greater length in a later section, entitled "Definition of Remuneration".

Vesting

Vesting refers to the time at which the employee becomes unconditionally entitled to the accrued pension, whether employment terminates before retirement age or not. Under federal and most provincial pension benefits legislation, benefits must vest after two years of plan membership.

In the case of the MP plan, vesting occurs after six years. However, before this a member is entitled to severance of six months' sessional indemnity, as well as a return of contributions with interest. We revisit this issue when we examine alternatives to the current arrangements.

Indexation

Most defined benefit plans in the public sector are fully indexed to the cost of living. The Quebec provincial plans are an exception; they are indexed at CPI minus 3 per cent. Meanwhile, some plans, such as OMERS, are partially indexed on a guaranteed basis and fully indexed if it becomes affordable; that is, pensioners receive ad hoc top-ups if the fund performs well.

Some plans in the private sector are indexed, but often up to a relatively low ceiling (e.g., 2 per cent, which was the formula under the CPP when it was first introduced). At current inflation rates, these plans are in fact providing full indexation, but this was not the case in the 1970s and 1980s, when inflation was occurring at a much higher rate than it is today. Other plans provide ad hoc increases, again often based on affordability. Appendix 3 gives the results of an informal internal survey by Mercer consultants; it is probably indicative of practices in larger defined benefit plans.

Given the current relatively low inflation rate, it does not seem necessary generally to revisit this issue. Also, the formula used in the MPs' plan (i.e., indexation delayed until age 60) is common among all federal plans that have particularly early unreduced retirement ages, e.g., the Canadian Forces and RCMP plans. If this formula is reviewed, it should be done for all these plans, not just the MP plan.

We return to this issue when reviewing public perceptions of MP pensions.

Investment of Funds

For federal pension plans, the investment issues are somewhat different from those discussed earlier in the comparison of defined benefit and defined contribution plans, as there is no external investment of funds. The government effectively invests in a passive portfolio of government bonds. While this investment is less volatile than market investment, it is generally considered less remunerative as well. However, because any superior performance or risk remains with the plan sponsor, these issues should be of no concern to plan members. We return to this issue when discussing an alternative defined contribution plan for members.

Taxation Issues

Registered pension plans and registered retirement savings plans are accorded very favourable tax treatment. Accordingly, the *Income Tax Act* puts a number of limits on pension plans and RRSPs to ensure that the tax advantages are not abused. In the case of registered plans, both employer and employee contributions can be used as deductions or credits for income tax purposes, while investment earnings on the pension or RRSP fund are not subject to income tax. Benefits are fully taxed as income when received. The tax limits on each type of plan are described briefly below.

Defined benefit plans

- maximum unit benefit — 2 per cent of final average earnings per year of service
- maximum benefit — $1722.22 per year of service to be indexed from 2005 (corresponding to a maximum salary of about $86,000 for members of a 2 per cent plan)
- minimum retirement age — 60, unless the member has more than 20 years' service
- various limitations on survivor benefits (the MP plan generally complies in this respect)
- members of a 2 per cent plan are generally precluded from contributing additional amounts to an RRSP

Defined contribution plans and RRSPs

- maximum annual contribution — 18 per cent of salary or $13,500 (corresponding to a salary of $75,000)
- this limit is slated to increase to $15,500 (corresponding to the same $86,000 as above) and to be indexed from 2005
- pension plan members can contribute 18 per cent of salary to RRSPs (subject to the $13,500 limit) minus a pension adjustment corresponding to the value of the pension plan

The RRSP room credited each year is cumulative. If no pension plan is in place and no RRSP contributions are made, the RRSP room can be used at any time in the future by making an RRSP contribution.

Also, if an employee is a member of a pension plan and the benefits do not vest, the RRSP room is restored (back to 1990) by way of a pension adjustment reversal (PAR). Therefore, a member of the MP plan would have no RRSP room during the membership period. However, if the Member left the House before accumulating six years of service, the RRSP room for this period would be restored.

Since the MP plan provides benefits that are 'offside', that is, benefits in excess of the 2 per cent unit and pensions before age 60 (some MPs may have sufficient service to qualify for an earlier retirement age under the *Income Tax Act*, but this is ignored under the registered plan), the offside benefits are provided through a retirement compensation arrangement (RCA). The RCA is designed effectively to neutralize the tax advantages of a registered pension plan, and it is therefore much more costly to fund benefits through an RCA than through a registered pension fund.

For example, the actuarial report on the MP plan to 31 March 1995 gives a total cost for 1997 of 12.3 per cent (8.4 per cent government, 3.9 per cent members) for the 2 per cent registered plan and 39.5 per cent (34.3 per cent government, 5.2 per cent members) for the RCA portion, which is the cost for the additional 2 per cent, plus pensions from age 55 to age 60. The cost difference is accounted for mostly by the RCA's unfavourable tax treatment.

The tax treatment explains why it would be very difficult to provide comparable levels of benefits under a defined contribution arrangement, unless the plan was exempt from *Income Tax Act* rules or the government was prepared to invest funds in a non-registered vehicle subject to unfavourable tax treatment. For example, if the government was prepared to invest the entire 52 per cent (43 per cent government, 9 per cent members) in a mix of RRSPs and an RCA, pensions at roughly the same level as the current plan could be provided, although as explained above, the distribution of benefits and risks would be different from the current plan. Public perceptions of such a move might not be favourable.

It should also be noted that pensions provided from registered pension plans can accrue only on taxable income. The definition of remuneration under the *Income Tax Act* excludes non-taxable allowances (like the incidental expense allowance available to members), so pension accruals cannot be based on such an allowance. If such allowances are grossed up and paid in a way that makes them taxable, however, pension benefits can be based on grossed-up taxable income.

Public Perceptions of Pension Plan Issues

Two issues relevant to a discussion of public service plans should be borne in mind:

- **Indexation.** All federal pension plans are fully indexed to increases in the CPI, although in the case of the MP plan, as well as some others, the commencement of indexation is delayed until age 60. While full or partial indexation of pensions is common in the public sector, guaranteed indexation it is less prevalent in private sector plans, where indexation is generally ad hoc, often depending on the performance of the pension fund and the affordability of pension increases. The magnitude of ad hoc increases is difficult to track, but they are estimated to cover about 50 per cent of CPI increases on average.
- **Pension plan coverage.** Coverage is virtually universal in the public sector. However, coverage in the private sector is less than 40 per cent of the workforce. If group RRSPs are included, the coverage figure would be slightly higher. While coverage tends to be greater among higher-paid employees, there are still considerable gaps in coverage, especially in the newer and emerging industries, such as high technology. Also, self-employed workers cannot belong to pension plans, although they can contribute to RRSPs.

Two issues identified as public irritants — early retirement with no minimum age and double dipping — were remedied, at least in part, by the 1995 amendments. First, pensions now start at age 55 at the earliest. While this is still relatively early, it is the age at which an unreduced pension can begin for a long-service public servant or member of the RCMP, for example. Second, pensions are now suspended if the recipient earns more than $5,000 a year from federal employment or a federal contract.

Public perceptions of pensions provided to public servants and to Members of Parliament in particular are generally unfavourable. Public perceptions tend to ignore the 'total compensation' approach, however, which recognizes that more generous pensions are offset by other elements of the compensation package, most importantly salary, which is likely less than the income most members could probably have earned in the private sector.

Some members of the public appear to find it objectionable that elected representatives have a plan that is considerably more generous than their own. Indeed, many working Canadians are not members of a plan at all; as many as 60 per cent of employees in the private sector do not belong to a pension plan, and those that are members are not generally entitled to generous indexed plans. Some Members of Parliament seem to have agreed with this assessment.

Members of public service plans say that they pay significant contributions for their benefits, and this is true. In the case of public servants, however, employee contributions cover about one-third of the total cost, while contributions by Members of Parliament cover only one-sixth of the cost.

One response to public perceptions has been to cancel the defined benefit plan altogether. British Columbia and Alberta have done this with regard to pensions for members of their respective legislatures, but not for those of public servants in general. Ontario has replaced the plan for MPPs with a considerably less generous defined contribution plan. This is a somewhat radical approach. Another solution in relation to the MPs' plan was suggested by the Sobeco report: replacement with a plan resembling the plan for ordinary public servants. However, this approach ignores the special circumstances of Members of Parliament discussed earlier.

In general, there may be grudging acceptance for the current plan, especially since it was amended to eliminate the most objectionable features, but any special deals for members (such as exemption from *Income Tax Act* rules) should be avoided.

In addition, the process for reviewing and revising members' benefits should not be perceived as self-serving. Changes should be based on a demonstrably sound rationale in relation to the specific situation of members and former members.

Delinking the Pension and Severance Allowance

As the pension plan was originally conceived, a pension would be payable immediately after a member with six years' service or more left the House. If the member had less than six years' service, a severance payment of six months' salary would be paid. Thus the career transition issue was handled, however imperfectly, by ensuring that departing members either had a pension or six months' salary. The 1995 amendments eliminated this relationship between the pension and the severance allowance, so that members who have not reached age 55 but are entitled to a deferred pension receive no immediate cash payment.

This could be remedied by extending a severance allowance or career transition benefit of six months' pay (or the number of months short of 55 for members who leave between $54\frac{1}{2}$ and 55) to all members who leave the House without being entitled to an immediate pension.

This would increase the cost of the severance allowance program to some extent.

Definition of Remuneration

As we have seen, MPs' remuneration consists of $64,400 in taxable salary and $21,300 (for most members) in non-taxable expense allowance. Grossing up the incidental expense allowance and adding it to members' salary would have several advantages:

- It would remove the irritant of having what is perceived as a portion of salary paid in non-taxable form — an opportunity not available to other Canadian taxpayers.
- It would allow the unit benefit for the pension to be reduced to 2.5 per cent, which is marginally above the 2 per cent unit prevalent in the public sector and in the generous private sector plans, rather than being twice as large.

There is no single gross-up factor, as tax rates depend on province of residence and family composition, as well as the use of various deductions and allowances (e.g., pension plan and/or RRSP contributions). We have assumed an Ontario taxpayer with a spouse and two dependent children. We have taken into account the 9 per cent pension contribution (on $64,400) and statutory deductions. The results are as follows:

	MPs		Senators	
	Current	Proposed	Current	Proposed
Taxable	$64,400	$106,010	$64,400	$83,806
Non-taxable	$21,300	nil	$10,100	nil
Total after-tax income	$64,928	$64,928	$54,467	$54,467

The next table compares the current approach with one based on a 2.5 per cent unit with a grossed-up taxable salary of $106,000 for members of the House of Commons, based on the same analysis as the preceding table (and rounded to the nearest $100). The same analysis is applied to the situation of senators later in the paper.

	Current Plan		Proposed Plan	
Taxable salary	$64,400		$106,000	
Benefit per year	4%	$2,576	2.5%	$2,650
Maximum benefit	75%	$48,300	70%	$74,200
Contribution per year	9%	$5,796	5.5%	$5,830
Government cost	42.7%	$5.9 million	18.7%	$4.3 million

The following observations can be made about these proposals:
- At present the maximum pension of 75 per cent of pre-retirement earnings is reached after 19 years of service. To be consistent, the proposed approach would have to limit pensions to about 47 per cent of grossed-up salary after 19 years. There is no rationale for limiting pensions to less than 50 per cent of salary in this context. We have therefore suggested that the limit be set at 70 per cent after 28 years, which is consistent with most other federal pension plans. It should be noted that
  - members' contributions would continue at the full level for 28 years; and
  - the probability of remaining an MP for 19 years is very low. To do so, an MP would have to be re-elected four or even five times. Given that the probability of returning to the House at each election is less than 60 per cent on average, there is about a 13 per cent probability of serving five terms and an 8 per cent probability of serving six terms.
- The government cost has been based on the 1997 normal cost figures in the actuarial report as of 31 March 1995, and the 1996 payroll of $13.9 million for sessional indemnities (excluding opted-out members). This translates into a payroll of $23 million for grossed-up equivalent salaries.

- Both the total cost as a percentage of salary and the government/portion have dropped more than *pro rata*. This is because the reduction occurs in the more expensive part of the RCA benefit, as compared to the more tax-effective, less costly registered benefit. This reduces the cost to the government in dollar terms.
- Pensions of 2 per cent per year on salaries of up to about $98,000 can be provided under the registered portion, and the balance under the RCA. We took both limits into account in estimating the 18.7 per cent cost of the proposed plan.

Opting In and Opting Out

Most pension plans have compulsory membership. While there is an element of paternalism in this, it also safeguards the interests of employers and employees. If opting out is permitted, no compensation is generally provided, and employees are expected to provide fully for their own retirement. If long-service employees have opted out but have made insufficient provision for retirement, the employer is in a quandary. Should the employer remind such retirees of their earlier decision to opt out of the plan and leave them to their own devices? Or should employer provide an *ex gratia* allowance, thereby signalling to other employees that benefits will eventually be available even if they do not join the plan? This is why membership in contributory plans is usually compulsory or plans are non-contributory, in which case the question never arises, as membership is automatic.

On the other hand, some plans provide optional features, where there is flexibility in regard to benefits and contributions. These plans are less paternalistic than the compulsory plans, but place responsibility on the employer to inform employees of the advantages and disadvantages of various options and make sure that employees provide adequately for their retirement, either within the plan or outside. For higher-paid employees, RRSP opportunities are relatively restricted, so it is often difficult to reproduce the level of retirement savings available within a plan through investment outside the plan.

Employers that sponsor pension plans with a 'traditional' design are coming under increasing pressure to change to a more modern design concept. Faced with the need to revise its pension plan, the plan sponsor would normally undertake an in-depth review to ascertain what type of plan design is most suitable for its employees. Once this was done, membership in the plan would normally be compulsory, possibly with some degree of flexibility for plan members. An alternative would be to maintain the current plan design but to modify it to adapt to changing circumstances.

Members of the 35th Parliament were allowed to opt out.[4] This option was not available to members of the 36th Parliament, but those who opted out in the 35th Parliament continue not to be members of the plan. No compensation was offered to members who opted out. Since they were not members of a registered plan, they were permitted to contribute 18 per cent of salary (or $11,592 based on the sessional indemnity of $64,400) to an RRSP. These contributions are fully tax deductible but must come from the member's own resources.

---

4   To be technically accurate, members were required to opt in, and those who did not do so were excluded from membership.

Several options are available to help members who have opted out to redress this situation and provide for their own retirement.

- They could be allowed to opt back in. This could be backdated to the beginning of the 36th Parliament, could commence as of 1 January 1998, or could be fully retroactive to the date they opted out.
- A permanent opt-out could be permitted, but some form of compensation could be provided to members who opted out.

These approaches are discussed further below.

Opt Back In

There is no particular problem with allowing an opt-in for service after 1 January 1997 (or 1 January 1998, if the necessary legislation is not introduced until 1998). Employee contributions could be collected for the full year, and benefits could begin to accrue from that date.

A retroactive change past January 1 of the year in which the change is made presents additional, but not insurmountable, problems. First, a decision will have to be made about the amount of employee contributions to be collected. This could be the regular contributions, or, if it were felt that some kind of penalty should be imposed for a late decision, twice the regular contributions could be charged. This is consistent with the charge for buying back service for certain types of past service or leave without pay in the public service plan.

Second, a past service pension adjustment (PSPA) would have to be calculated. This PSPA eliminates the possibility of double dipping in regard to tax-assisted retirement savings. In other words, the member could not retain an RRSP for years in question while benefiting from a tax-assisted pension plan for the same years. Members who contributed the maximum amount to an RRSP would have to transfer this to the MPs' plan as part of their past service contribution and/or withdraw the RRSP contributions and pay tax on the withdrawal.

An alternative to permitting the member to purchase the full 4 per cent benefit would be to permit buy-back in the registered plan only, i.e., a 2 per cent benefit with normal retirement at age 60. Again, this could be seen as imposing a penalty for making a late election to join the plan. The employee contribution to the registered plan is set at 4 per cent, so the member would have to contribute this amount or double this amount if that were the decision. A PSPA would be imposed as discussed above, i.e., a complete reversal of the 18 per cent per year RRSP room for the years during which the member was not a member of the plan.

Although these members may believe that the proposed approach (a 2.5 per cent benefit on the grossed-up salary) would have been acceptable at the time, whereas the 4 per cent plan was not, it would be difficult to implement this change retroactively, and we recommend against it, as it would mean re-filing many income tax returns.

If these members wished to remain opted out — that is, not to rejoin the regular plan — it would be possible to compensate them for future service. In so far as past service is concerned, it would be possible to provide this in a manner similar to that described above, that is, on a defined benefit basis only. If it were decided to provide a defined contribution plan as the alternative plan, it is recommended that compensation not be provided for past service. While such compensation could be paid (for example, through the RCA), it would not be in accordance with the registered pension plan provisions of the *Income Tax Act*. These permit past service to be credited on a defined benefit, but not a defined contribution basis. It is assumed that any changes proposed should generally be in compliance with the *Income Tax Act*.

Permanent Opt-Out

Although this would not be consistent with other federal pension plans, a permanent opting-out provision could be contemplated. By this, we mean that all Members of Parliament, including new members as they are elected, would be given the choice of opting out, rather than making opting out a one-time opportunity, as was the case for the 35th Parliament. Again, this choice could be provided with no compensation, but it is clearly onerous for members to provide for their own retirement through RRSPs. As discussed above, it would be possible to provide complete compensation, by a combination of RRSPs and an RCA provided by the government, but it would be difficult to see the rationale for this — it would be preferable in this case to require compulsory membership.

The alternative plan could be either a defined benefit plan or a defined contribution plan. Since the alternative approach suggested here is only marginally more generous than the typical public service plan, however, there would not be enough to distinguish the proposed plan from the *Public Service Superannuation Act* plan. We therefore propose that the alternative plan be a defined contribution plan, in line with those in the private sector. One design might be to have the government match members' contributions to an RRSP on a one-for-one-basis. That is, if the member contributed up to 5.5 per cent of the grossed-up salary to an RRSP, the government would match this amount. (This percentage was chosen to be consistent with the level of member contributions proposed for the defined benefit plan. A level of 4 to 5 per cent would be typical in a private sector defined contribution plan.) A way would have to be found to lock in these funds; otherwise the arrangement would amount to a 5.5 per cent salary increase, not a retirement fund.

Under this model, the government contribution would vest immediately, i.e., would immediately become the property of the member, even though it was locked in. This would be a departure from the six years required to qualify for a pension under the current plan but is more in line with the practices of defined contribution plans.

Alternatively, a defined contribution plan could be set up. This could require two-year vesting if the plan complied with pension legislation. However, since MPs' employment is exempt from compliance with federal standards, a six-year vesting period could be imposed (but see below for more discussion of this issue).

If such a plan were set up, it would probably be advantageous to have it invested externally so that members could choose the investment mix. This would be a significant departure from current federal pension plans, as all funds to date have been invested in non-negotiable government of Canada bonds. However, all the current plans are defined benefit plans, where the investment performance of the funds does not affect the benefits received by plan members.

The table in Appendix 2 indicates relative levels of benefits for the regular plan as compared to the defined contribution plan suggested here. As the table shows, the level of benefits is considerably below that available under the regular plan.

We have assumed that the defined contribution plan would be limited to 28 years of service, to be consistent with the defined benefit plan.

Finally, with regard to vesting, since we have recommended that the pension and the severance allowance be delinked, it is possible to suggest a different vesting period than the six-year period under the current plan.

According to the actuarial report, the probability of re-election varies between 35 per cent and 75 per cent, depending on age. It is probably lower for first-time members. Therefore, a plan with a six-year vesting period, even though it is very generous, is a high-risk proposition. Since at least one re-election is required to qualify for a pension, a high proportion of members will not meet this minimum qualification.

A less generous plan can be provided at lower risk. A defined contribution plan, if it is implemented, could have two-year vesting. This is tantamount to immediate vesting, as the probability that a member will leave the House in the first two years after an election is very low.

For consistency, however, most other terms of the defined benefit plan should be imposed on the defined contribution plan:

- no payment of pension until age 55 or departure from the House of Commons, whichever is later; and
- 60 per cent joint and survivor benefits for members who have an eligible spouse at the time they leave the House.

The defined contribution plan should also be portable to another pension plan or RRSP, subject to the same conditions.

It would be impossible, however, to impose some of the other conditions of the defined benefit plan because of constraints on the market for annuities. The non-reproducible conditions include

- indexation;
- benefits for surviving children; and
- suspension of pension on re-election or acceptance of federal employment.

A transitional issue arises in respect of members who now belong to the regular plan and but might wish to opt out under the circumstances described above. If they have more than six years' service, they are currently vested, so a value for this service could be calculated on an actuarial basis and paid into their defined contribution account. Alternatively, the benefit could be frozen at the number of years of service on the date of opt-out and paid as a pension once the member has left the House. The former solution is not recommended, in the light of the public reaction to such a move when the Ontario MPP plan was replaced by a defined contribution plan.

For those with less than six years' service, it might be expedient to have them join the alternative plan retroactive to their initial date of election.

We suggest that a once-only opportunity be given to opt in or opt out. Members now opted out could opt in, but this decision would be irrevocable. Current members would likewise have an opportunity to opt out irrevocably. Finally, new members could be given a once-only chance to join.

These proposals are summarized in the accompanying table.

Wish to opt out for future	Opted Out in 35th Parliament	
	Yes	**No**
Yes	• alternative pension plan for future service • no buy-back of past service	• alternative pension plan for future service • more than six years' service: defined benefit for accrued service • less than six years' service: membership in alternative plan retroactive to date of election
No	• defined benefit for future service • opportunity to buy back past service on defined benefit basis (terms to be determined)	• defined benefit for all service

It would also be possible to give members who opted out in the 35th Parliament a taxable lump sum to compensate them for not belonging to the plan for this period. As noted before, unused RRSP room since 1990 is cumulative, so if the member had not been making RRSP contributions, some or all of this lump sum could be tax-sheltered.

It should be emphasized, however, that no additional RRSP room could be made available to such members without going outside the *Income Tax Act* rules. Also, the public perception and accountability issues surrounding such a proposal should be examined carefully.

Senators

The same approach should be taken to the salary and allowances of members of the Senate and hence to benefit accruals and contribution rate. Senators' sessional indemnity and allowances should be replaced by a taxable salary of $83,800, which translates to an accrual rate of 2.3 per cent and a contribution rate of 5.4 per cent, as compared to the current rates of 3 per cent and 7 per cent respectively. (It might be convenient to round the contribution rate up to 5.5 per cent.)

Concerning the limit on total pension, we recommend that the maximum period of 25 years be retained, for a total maximum replacement ratio of 57.5 per cent, so as not to increase benefits for longer-service senators, given the much higher probability of senators remaining in Parliament for longer periods than is normally the case for members of the House of Commons.

The proposed changes would reduce costs to the government somewhat, given that the reduction would come mainly from the more costly RCA portion.

Alternatives to a Pension Plan

A pension plan is an extremely tax-efficient way of providing retirement income. In the case of the MPs' plan, it is particularly advantageous, as the government bears the full cost of the 'offside' benefits, that is, the additional 2 per cent benefit above that permitted under the *Income Tax Act* for registered plans, as well as benefits payable before age 60. To reproduce these benefits without using the current pension plan vehicle would require a taxable salary increase of more than 50 per cent.

Some limited tax room is available through the retiring allowance route. Up to $2,000 per year of service before 1996, with an additional $1,500 for each year before 1989 during which the employee was not a member of a registered pension plan, can be tax sheltered. However, this is a small amount compared to the $30,000 to $35,000 per year on average required to provide the pension benefit. Also, this tax-free rollover has been eliminated for service after 1996. In the end, its usefulness for future accruals is nil.

The general conclusion is, therefore, that there is no alternative to a pension plan for providing a benefit of the magnitude of the benefit under the current plan. RRSPs or an equivalent approach have some limited usefulness in providing a partial replacement for the benefit, as discussed earlier in the paper.

Benefit Plans: Findings and Trends

Overview

Provincial Governments

- The MPs' benefit program is superior, being particularly more generous in the health, dental and vision care plans.
- The main reason is cost-sharing.

Crown Corporations

- MPs' benefits are comparable (and often similar) in design, scope and cost-sharing.
- In some cases, Crown corporations provide better co-insurance (reimbursement level) for health and dental.

'Other' Public Sector

- The MPs' benefit program is mid-range but overall provides equivalent benefits.
- The MPs' benefit program is more generous in cost-sharing than that of many organizations.

Private Sector

- MPs' benefits are equal to or slightly more generous than the 'typical' private sector program.
- The private sector is increasingly moving away from 'typical' programs to approaches that give plan members more choice, flexibility, and tax-effectiveness.

Summary

- The suite of benefits available to MPs is, on the whole, competitive with those offered employees in the other sectors examined, although the degree of competitiveness varies.
- The program is somewhat more generous than those of the provinces.
- The program is somewhat less generous when compared to Crown corporations.
- The program compares favourably with the 'traditional' private sector but lags somewhat behind private sector trends (e.g., choice, flexibility, tax-effectiveness).

Trends

We understand that there may be perceptions that MPs' benefits are less generous than those MPs may have enjoyed while employed before being elected.

Overall, as our comparison indicates, the benefits program is neither overly generous nor deficient in relation to the plans with which we compared it.

Perceptions to the contrary may be attributable in part to comparing the MPs' plan with private-sector benefit plans that have moved away from traditional designs to the newer approach of offering participants choice and flexibility. Flexible benefit programs in particular are coming into vogue in the private sector for reasons that include

- the changing social/employment promise,
- new demographics realities,
- legal/legislative intrusion,
- cost shifting/cost containment,
- employees' changing needs,
- tax-effectiveness,
- competitive pressures, and
- the total compensation approach.

MPs' existing benefit program is a 'traditional' plan. It offers little choice or flexibility. It was designed from a paternalistic perspective; as a result, for reasons similar to those just listed, some members may not see it as ideal or even appropriate to their needs and those of their families in today's environment.

This may be part of the reason for some members' views on the relative generosity of the benefits program. If this is the situation, and if circumstances permit, a review of the *raison d'être* of the current program and an examination of less traditional approaches, including, for example, flexible benefits and health services spending accounts, may be appropriate.

Other Observations

The Manual of Allowances and Services, Volume II (published under the authority of the Board of Internal Economy, House of Commons), details members' benefits and indemnities thoroughly and comprehensively but is not particularly user-friendly. This too could be fuelling some of the perceptions about the benefits program.

Consideration could be given to providing Members with readable, easy-to-understand benefits program information, as is common in the private sector. For example,

- benefits at a glance
- personalized comprehensive benefits statements
- on-line (real-time) access through electronic media

The information about sick leave, for example, is vague, and there is no obvious link between this benefit and long-term disability. Chapter F-1. A, Section C.c, Sessional Allowance and Expense Allowance, deals with sick leave. This brief reference is further linked to Section D, Attendance Forms. But neither reference appears to be linked to Chapter F-3, Insurance Plans, where there is a (not so obvious) link to long-term disability (LTD). The LTD plan has a 13-week qualifying period for eligibility. Therefore, one assumes that sick leave is payable for a maximum of 13 weeks.

If a member does not qualify for LTD, however, for how long would sick leave benefits be paid? The manual does not specify.

To summarize, sick leave is an important benefit to members (and a potentially expensive one), and a clear sick leave policy (entitlements and procedures), including its integration with long-term disability, should be developed and communicated effectively.

Proposals

As in the case of pensions, we were not able to undertake an in-depth needs analysis. However, after reviewing trends for employee groups comparable to MPs, we would recommend that a move to a more flexible benefits program, giving members greater latitude to choose benefits that suit their personal and family situations, be explored. We recognize that such a move could be contemplated only if such changes were implemented for government employees at the same time. Again, it is important to ensure that any such changes are made within the current fiscal envelope devoted to members' benefits.

We also suggest that the sick leave provisions be clarified and properly documented, to ensure that the application of these provisions is consistent with the long-term disability plan, is comparable to such plans for comparator groups, and takes into account the special circumstances of MPs (e.g., failure to be re-elected while on disability status).

Consideration should also be given to providing more user-friendly communication of these programs and policies.

Conclusions

Based on the preceding analysis, our conclusions and findings are as follows.

Pension Plan

- The pension plan for Members of Parliament, while appearing generous, is not necessarily out of line with public and private sector plans that recognize the impact of the mid-career hire aspect of the career path of their senior employees.
- We did not examine the total compensation of members, so it is difficult to say whether the pension plan makes up for other elements of the compensation package that are inferior to those for groups with which we compared them.
- The cost of reproducing the current pension plan would be about 50 per cent of the sessional indemnity.
- Pension plans examined in Sobeco's international comparison have not changed since 1994.
- However, a number of plans for members of provincial legislatures have been cancelled altogether or replaced by defined contribution plans.
- It is not recommended that the current pension plan be replaced by a defined contribution plan or other arrangement (e.g., salary in lieu).
- The incidental expense allowance should be grossed up for tax and included as part of pensionable salary. The unit benefit and member contribution rates should then be reduced to 2.5 per cent and 5.5 per cent respectively, for up to 28 years.
- The current plan (modified as outlined in this report) should be retained for those who wish to continue to participate in it.
- The current indexing formula should be retained.
- The severance allowance should be separated from the pension plan — it should be payable to all departing members not entitled to an immediate pension.
- A permanent opting-out feature could be offered to members who are uncomfortable belonging to a plan that is significantly more generous than the retirement arrangements of most of their constituents.
- In the event that opting out is permitted, there could be some partial compensation by establishing an alternative defined contribution pension plan that members would be able to join.
- Members who opted out could be given the choice of opting into the regular plan, in which case benefits for past service could be granted to them on the full or partial payment of employee contributions.
- If members who have opted out wish to continue in the alternative plan, buy-back of past service should not be permitted.
- Any lump sum compensation given to such members should not be given special income tax treatment.
- Members who belong to the regular plan who wish to opt out should retain the defined benefit formula for years of service to date, or if they now have less than six years' service, they should join the alternative plan retroactive to their date of election.

- Senators' salary and allowances and hence pension accruals and contribution rates should be change in the same way as proposed for members of the House of Commons; that is, a unit of 2.3 per cent per year and an contribution rate of 5.5 per cent for a maximum of 25 years.

Benefits

- The MPs' benefit plan is in line with or slightly more generous than that of comparison groups.
- The plan is not keeping up with recent private sector trends. This may be the source of some of the dissatisfaction expressed by members.
- Benefit plans should be reviewed and modernized at the same time as plans covering executives in the public service are reviewed.
- The application of sick leave provisions (and their communication to members) should be reviewed.
- More user-friendly communication material on benefits plans should be produced for members.

Appendix 1

Summary of Benefits and Costs

Service from 13 July 1996

Benefit accrual rate	MPRA	RCA	Total
Benefit paid from age 55 to 60	0	4%	4%
Benefit paid from age 60	2%	2%	4%
Benefit accrued after age 71	0	4%	4%
Maximum accrual			75%
Member contributions			
• less than age 71, below *Income Tax Act* maximum	4%	5%	9%
• otherwise	0	9%	9%
Benefit costs			
Total normal cost	12.3%	39.5%	51.8%
Member portion	3.9%	5.2%	9.1%
Government portion	8.4%	34.3%	42.7%

Benefit Provisions

Average period: six highest consecutive years of earnings

Survivor benefits:
- Spouse — 60 per cent of member's pension
- Eligible children — 10 per cent of member's pension, if there is a surviving spouse, 20 per cent otherwise (maximum, 30 per cent and 80 per cent respectively)

Indexation: CPI increases, delayed to age 60, at which point pension increased to reflect cumulative increases since leaving House (no delay for survivors or disabled pensioners)

Minimum age to commence pension: Age 55

Entitlement to pension: 6 years' service (otherwise, return of contributions)

Notes:

- The MPRA account is for benefits that comply with the *Income Tax Act*. It is operated as a registered pension fund (i.e., no tax on investment income).
- The RCA is for benefits that do not so comply. Contributions and investment income are subject to a refundable excise tax of 50 per cent.
- Actuarial costs are extracted from the Actuarial Report as at 31 March 1995 of the Pension Plan for Members of Parliament. Figures given here are for the plan year 1997, which is the first full year for which the revised benefits are in effect. They ignore any reduction that may occur because of the surplus in the account.
- As noted in the paper, members of the 35th Parliament had the option of opting out.
- Pensioners who re-enter the House of Commons or are appointed to the Senate have their pensions suspended.
- Pensioners receiving remuneration of more than $5,000 in any year as a federal employee or under a federal contract have their pension reduced by the amount of such remuneration.
- Benefits under a registered plan cannot accrue past age 69. This was changed recently from age 71, which is reflected above. Presumably, this change will be implemented eventually in the MPRA. It will not have a material impact on total costs.
- Member contributions drop to 1 per cent once the full 75 per cent benefit has been accrued.

Appendix 2

Benefit and Cost Comparison, Defined Benefit and Defined Contribution Plans

The table on this page compares the benefits at retirement and actuarial costs for 'typical' members under the current and proposed defined benefit plans and the proposed defined contribution plan.

Note that we have not taken the adverse tax effects of an RCA into account. Therefore, these figures would be more comparable to those in the Sobeco report, rather than those in the actuarial report. The defined contribution plan could be provided entirely within a registered pension plan.

The RCA treatment of the 'offside' benefits increases total cost by about 50 per cent. Therefore, Member C, for example, who represents the 'average' member, would give rise to a cost of about 54 per cent (under the current defined benefit plan) using the actuarial report basis.

Note that the proposed defined benefit plan is the same as the current defined benefit plan, except that it is based on an accrual rate of 2.5 per cent of the grossed-up salary, to a maximum of 70 per cent. The proposed defined contribution plan is based on a 5.5 per cent member contribution plus a 5.5 per cent government contribution, again on the grossed-up salary.

Data				
Member	Age at entry	Age at exit	Service	Sex
A	30	49	19	M
B	40	50	10	F
C	45	60	15	M
D	30	60	30	M

Results												
Member	Current Defined Benefit Plan				Proposed Defined Benefit Plan				Defined Contribution Plan			
	Pension 1997 $	Total cost[1]	Er cost	Ee cost	Pension 1997 $	Total cost	Er cost	Ee cost	Pension 1997 $	Total cost	Er cost	Ee cost
A	44,919	27.6%	18.6%	9.0%	46,209	17.2%	11.7%	5.5%	25,055	11.0%	.5%	5.5%
B	23,957	36.6%	27.6%	9.0%	24,645	22.9%	17.4%	5.5%	10,336	11.0%	5.5%	5.5%
C	35,9354	2.1%	33.1%	9.0%	36,967	26.7%	20.8%	5.5%	13,702	11.0%	5.5%	5.5%
D	44,919	18.8%	12.0%	6.8%	69,006	17.5%	12.2%	5.3%	34,865	10.4%	5.2%	5.2%

Er = Employer cost; Ee = Employee cost
Note: Costs are shown as a percentage of salary for the member's entire career.

Replacement Ratio

The next tables show the replacement ratio, that is, the pension at exit as a percentage of the average salary.

Member	Years of Service	Current Defined Benefit Plan (based on sessional indemnity)	Proposed Plan (based on grossed-up salary)	Defined Contribution Plan (based on grossed-up salary)
A	19	75%	46.9%	23.6%
B	10	40%	25.0%	9.8%
C	15	60%	37.5%	12.9%
D	30	75%	70.0%	32.9%

Actuarial Assumptions

Interest rate:
- defined benefit plan, 7%
- defined contribution plan, 6.5%

Inflation: 3%

Future salary increases: 3%

Mortality after retirement: GAM83 (standard industry table)

Family composition: Married, female spouse 3 years younger than male spouse

Notes:
1. The differential between the interest rates for the defined benefit and defined contribution plans simulates the more efficient investment expected under the former type of plan.
2. Defined contribution benefits are assumed to be paid on the same basis as the defined benefit plan.

Appendix 3

Results of Survey on Post-Retirement Indexation

The results are based on an informal survey of Mercer consultants in regard to plans that provide automatic and/or ad hoc indexation. The survey did not indicate the percentage of all plans that provide some form of indexation.

Total number of plans included in survey: 100
1. 68 per cent of plans provide indexation on an ad hoc basis.
2. Indexation formula:
   - 94 per cent of plans use a CPI-related formula
   - number of plans with a CPI-related formula subject to a minimum or maximum:

	Ad hoc	Automatic	Total
Minimum	5	2	7
Maximum	7	19	26

   - Proportion of inflation protection covered:

% of CPI	Number (%) of plans				
	Ad hoc		Automatic		Total
50%[1]	36	(53%)	5	(16%)	41
51% - 60%	6	(9%)	1	(3%)	7
61% - 70%	6	(9%)	0	(0%)	6
71% - 80%	3	(4%)	10	(31%)	13
100%	11	(16%)	10	(31%)	21
Cannot be determined[2]	6	(9%)	6	(19%)	12
Total	68	(100%)	32	(100%)	100
Average % of CPI	63%		79%		68%
Median % of CPI	50%		80%		60%

Notes:
1. All 50 per cent except one with 33 per cent (automatic).
2. Indexation formula could be a fixed percentage, a fixed dollar amount, an offset formula, etc.

3. 80 per cent of plans provide post-retirement indexation to former deferred vested members (82 per cent for ad hocs and 75 per cent for automatic).
4. Frequency of indexation:

	Number (%) of plans				
	Ad hoc		Automatic		Total
1 year	30	(44%)	31	(97%)	61
2 years	9	(13%)	-	-	9
3 years	23	(34%)	1	(3%)	24
More than 3 years	5	(7%)	-	-	5
Not indicated	1	(2%)	-	-	1
Total	68	(100%)	32	(100%)	100
Average frequency	2.1 years		1 year		1.8 years

Appendix 4

Survey of Provincial Legislatures' Pension Plans

For this survey of the pension plans available to members of provincial legislatures, changes since the 1993 situation (described in the Sobeco report) are noted, and a summary of the amended provisions is provided, where applicable and available.

British Columbia

Effective 19 June 1996, there is no active pension accrual under the plan as described in the Sobeco report. However, pensions being paid and accruals before 19 June 1996 will be paid according to the terms of the plan as described in the Sobeco report.

Effective 19 June 1996, pension accrual ceased under a July 1995 amendment to the *Legislative Assembly Allowances and Pension Act* (LAAPA). At that time, it was determined that members who did not meet the vesting requirements (seven years of service or service through more than two parliaments) on that date would not receive a pension when they ceased to be members. Those who were members on June 19, 1996 and vested would receive a pension under the LAAPA when they ceased to be members, reached age 55, or their age plus service equalled 60 or more.

Under a further amendment of 28 July 1997 (Bill 51), members who were not vested as of 19 June 1996 will be eligible to receive a pension under the LAPPA once their total service (including periods after 19 June 1996) totals seven years or more than two parliaments. Bill 51 also amended the *Legislative Assembly Management Committee Act*, giving the committee the power to establish a voluntary group RRSP for members of the legislative assembly with effect from as early as 19 June 1996. A group RRSP is now being set up, but details are not yet available.

Alberta

At present there is no active participation in a pension plan or RRSP for members of Alberta's legislative assembly. Effective 14 June 1993, the *Members of the Legislative Assembly Pension Plan Act* (MLAPPA) was amended. Members who had at least five years of service and former members will receive a pension under the terms of the MLAPPA for service before 14 June 1993. According to the legislative assembly office, no substitute pension plan or RRSP is in place.

Saskatchewan

The *Members of the Legislative Assembly Superannuation Act* (MLASA) has remained largely unchanged since 1979 when the plan was converted from a defined benefit plan to a defined contribution plan (contributions 9 per cent of salary, matched by the province, with additional non-matched contributions by the member permitted). Changes to the MLASA effective in July 1995, were as follows.

- A maximum for pensions to be paid to defined benefit members who were in active service in 1995, equal to 70 per cent of the average annual indemnity, and additional allowance based on the best four years' salary were introduced.
- A special allowance for holding the office of premier was eliminated.
- For both defined benefit and defined contribution members, the MLASA was amended to allow for portability and to restrict double dipping when members are employed either in Saskatchewan or federally in a public office.

Manitoba

The *Legislative Assembly Act* was amended in December 1993 by regulation retroactive to 1 January 1992. The terms of the plan have not changed since that time.

Ontario

Ontario's *Legislative Assembly Retirement Allowances Act* (LARAA) was repealed and replaced with the *MPP Pension Act, 1996* (MPPA) on 25 April. Further amendments received royal assent on 9 December 1996. The MPPA changed the benefit formula effective 1 January 1992 to comply with the *Income Tax Act* regulations for registered plans and converted the plan to a non-contributory defined contribution plan effective 8 June 1995. For service before 8 June 1995, the plan is a defined benefit plan, and members can choose to convert their defined benefit accruals to the defined contribution plan. The conversion value and the benefits paid if the member elects to remain under the defined benefit provisions are calculated based on the plan outlined in the Sobeco report for periods of service before 1992. For periods of service between 1 January 1992 and 8 June 1995, the MPPA provides for benefits under both a registered and a supplementary plan as outlined below.

Registered Plan

Vesting remains at five years of service, and the earliest date for receipt of a pension remains age plus service equal to 55. The *Income Tax Act* minimum reduction for pensions received before age 60 is explicit in the MPPA.

Benefit accrual for pre-1992 service under the registered plan appears to mirror the provisions outlined in the Sobeco report, with the exception that the indexation and increases in the LARAA as it read on 31 December 1991 do not apply. Benefit accrual under the registered plan for service between 1 January 1992 and 8 June 1995 is based on the *Income Tax Act* regulation defined benefit accrual limit: 2 per cent of the best three years of indexed salary multiplied by years of service in this period.

The maximum for pension accrued under the registered plan is 5 per cent of the best 36 months of salary per year of pre-8 June 1995 service, to a maximum of 75 per cent of the member's best 36 months of salary.

Death benefits under the MPPA are the sum of the death benefit for pre-1992 service and the death benefit for service between 1 January 1992 and 8 June 1995. For pre-1992 service, the death benefits remains as outlined in the Sobeco report (60 per cent for the member's spouse plus 10 per cent for each of the member's children, to a maximum of three children). For service between 1 January 1992 and 8 June 1995, the spousal death benefit is 66 per cent of the member's pension for this period, and there is no provision for a member's children unless there is no spouse at the time of the member's death.

The indexation factor for pre-1992 service remains as outlined in the Sobeco report. For post-1991 service, there is full CPI indexing.

Members continued to be required to contribute 10 per cent of salary until 8 June 1995.

Supplementary Plan

The MPPA also established a supplementary plan under which a member's pension is equal to 5 per cent of the best 36 months of service multiplied by years of service to 8 June 1995 (to a maximum of 15 years) minus the amount received under the registered plan.

Quebec

The pensions of members of the National Assembly are governed by the *Conditions of Employment and Pension Plan of the Members of the National Assembly Act*. There have not been significant changes to the act since 1992. The summary of the plan provided in the Sobeco report remains accurate.

New Brunswick

The *Members' Pension Act* took effect on 10 December 1993 and has not changed substantially since then. (In 1997 there were technical amendments that provided for division of pension benefits on marriage breakdown.)

Nova Scotia

The *Members' Retiring Allowances Act* was amended in November 1993 to change the service buy-back provisions, to introduce an early retirement pension payable at age 45 but reduced by 0.5 per cent for each month the member is under age 55 (limited to a 50 per cent reduction), and to split the pension to be received into a registered pension subject to the *Income Tax Act* and a supplementary plan.

Prince Edward Island

The pension plan for members of the Prince Edward Island legislative assembly has been amended twice since 1993. In May 1994, the *Legislative Assembly Retirement Allowances Act* (LARAA) was passed. The LARAA made changes, retroactive to 1971, to the pension plan established under the *Legislative and Executive Pensions Act*. The amendments included a reduction in members' contribution levels from 8.5 per cent to 6.5 per cent and a reduction of the indexation factor to CPI minus 2 per cent.

The benefit formula in the LARAA is 75 per cent of a member's total contributions; thus, pensions accrued between 1971 and 1994 were reduced, effective in 1994, as a result of the reduction in members' contribution levels.

A new plan is now in place, established as a result of a report by an independent commission.

Newfoundland

The *Members of the House of Assembly Pensions Act* was enacted in 1975. The only significant change since 1993 was an amendment to the 75 per cent maximum pension section, enacted in 1981, providing that it was to have prospective effect from 1981 only.

Appendix 5

International Comparisons

This appendix is based on the Sobeco report, with our corrections and additions.

	Australia	Belgium	France*	Sweden**	United Kingdom	United States
Right to pension	12 years' service or age 60 (or involuntary leave) and 8 years' service	Immediate vesting	Immediate vesting	6 years' service and age 50 (members leaving before this age receive no retirement benefits from the plan)	Immediate vesting	5 years' service
Unreduced pension	12 years' service or age 60 (or involuntary leave) and 8 years' service	8 years' service, age 55 or less than 8 years' service, from date of payment of other pension benefits	age 55 (less one year per child for women)	age 65	age 65 or age 60 if age + service = 80	age 62 or age 50 and 20 years' service or 25 years' service
Retirement before unreduced pension	Lump sum of either 2 or 3 times employee contributions (depending on circumstances)	• 8 years' service, after age 52, immediate pension reduced 5% per year • 8 years' service, before age 52, deferred pension at age 52 (reduced) or age 55 (unreduced) • less than 8 years' service, deferred pension payable from date of payment of other pension benefits	• deferred pension at age 55 • indexed before retirement • early retirement from age 50 with reduction factor	no pension payable; only transitional benefits	deferred pension at age 65 or greater of age 60 and age = 80 - service indexed before retirement	age 55 and 10 years' service: immediate pension reduced 5% per year before age 62 before: deferred pension at age 62

	Australia	Belgium	France*	Sweden**	United Kingdom	United States
Amount of pension	50% + 2.5% for each year of service after 8 times parliamentary allowance + 6.25% of additional salary for each year of service in a higher office	3.75% of final salary for each year of service	4.5% of final salary for each of the first 15 years of service, 2.25% thereafter	12 or more years: 11.5% up to 7.5 times base (about $48,000), plus 65% of excess 6 to 11 years, pro-rated on service	2% of terminal pensionable salary + 3% of remuneration exceeding pensionable salary for each year of service	1.7% - high-3 salary for years of service before 20 +1.0% - high-3 salary for years of service after 20 + pension provided by Thrift Savings Plan
Bridging benefits	—	—	—	—	—	• if retired with unreduced pension • approximately equal to social security • payable to age 62
Maximum pension	75% of salary	75% of final salary	84.375% of final salary	65% of high-5 salary	2/3 of terminal salary	—
Post-retirement increases	at salary growth rate	at salary growth rate	at salary growth rate	100% of CPI	100% of CPI	• CPI minus 1%, if CPI greater than 3% • CPI or 2%, whichever is less, if CPI less than 3% • applicable from age 62, or any age for disabled or survivor
Death benefit • after retirement	83.3% spousal pension	60% spousal pension + 6% for each child	60% spousal pension + 6% for each child		62.5% spousal pension + 37.5% for each child	50% spousal pension (but member's pension reduced by 10% while both alive) + children's benefit

	Australia	Belgium	France*	Sweden**	United Kingdom	United States
Death benefit • before retirement	immediate spousal pension of 83.3% of credited pension calculated as if 8 years' service if less than 8	immediate spousal pension of 60% of credited pension calculated as if members had 8 years of service if less than 8 + 6% for each child	immediate spousal pension of 60% of credited pension		twice annual salary	as above, if member has 10 years of service (otherwise, a lump sum is payable)
Members' contributions	• 11.5% of parliamentary allowance before 18 years' service • 5.75% of parliamentary allowance after 18 years' service • 11.5% of additional salary before maximum pension is reached • 5.75% if additional salary after maximum pension is reached	7.5% of salary	7.85% of salary	0%	6% of pensionable salary + 9% of additional salary	1.3% of salary + up to 10% of salary to Thrift Savings Plan (matched by government at 100% up to 5%)

* Based on Mercer interpretation of information received from the National Assembly.
** See additional information on Sweden after this table.

Sweden

In the case of Sweden, no pension is payable before age 65, but there is a *guarantee of no loss of income*, from the time of leaving Parliament to age 65.

The conditions for the guarantee are as follows:

- Benefit ceases if member returns to Parliament.
- No guarantee if term in Parliament less than three years.
- The guarantee is one year if term in Parliament was less than six years but more than three years.
- For members with more than six years' service, the time limit on the guarantee is as follows:
  - two years, if less than age 40,
  - five years, if aged 40 to 50, and
  - to age 65 if older than 50.
- The guarantee is 80% of sessional indemnity for the first year after leaving Parliament.
- 5.5% per year of service in following years: minimum 33% (six years' service), maximum 66% (12 years' service.)
- Amount paid is reduced by all other income earned.

Appendix 6

CEO-Specific Plan Provisions

The survey indicates that of the 232 plans recorded, 27 (12 per cent) were intended specifically for chief executive officers. The typical provisions of these plans, as compared to those for members of the House of Commons and deputy ministers in the federal public service, are shown in the accompanying table.

	MP plan	Federal DM plan	Survey
accrual rate	4%	2%	over 2%: 20% 2%: 56% 1.5 to 2%: 12% under 1.5%: 12%
maximum service	19 years	10 years	varies
averaging period	6 years	6 years	1 - 5 years
pensionable earnings	sessional indemnity	salary plus bonus	salary only: 45% salary plus bonus: 55%
early retirement	age 55	60, 55 and 30 years service	55-62
benefits to surviving spouse	60% joint & survivor	50% joint & survivor	joint & survivor in about 65% of cases other form of benefit in about 35% of cases
Indexation	100% CPI, delayed to age 60	100% CPI	automatic: 20% ad hoc: 10% none: 70%
employee contribution	9%	non-contributory	no contribution to basic plan, contribution capped: 80% contribution on full salary: 20%
funding	internal government bonds, includes RCA for off-side benefits	pay as you go	not funded: 50-55% RCA: 30% secured, other: 15%
basic plan	n/a	PSSA	varies, depending on sector

Appendix 7
Transitional Arrangements for the Proposed Defined Benefit Plan

Since the pension benefit under the defined benefit plan is calculated by multiplying the six-year average sessional indemnity on leaving the House by the number of years of service and by the accrual rate, a change in both the indemnity and the rate will give rise to some transitional issues for current members. There is also the question of the limit on years of service. Some of these issues are technicalities, while others are more substantive.

Option 1: 'Grandparent' Current Members

Under this option, the current rate would continue to be 4 per cent, and the notional sessional indemnity for years after 1997 would be, say, 60 per cent of the actual sessional indemnity ($64,400 ÷ $106,000 = 60.8%). Pensions would continue to be limited to 75 per cent of the old-style sessional indemnity after 19 years of service (which some members have already reached).

Only members elected in the 36th (1997) and subsequent parliaments would receive pensions based on the new formula.

This is not really satisfactory, as it means running two parallel plans for many years and calculating notional old-style sessional indemnities into the future. Nor does it really address the public perception issue presented by the 4 per cent accrual rate for current members.

Option 2: Apply New Accrual Rate to All Years of Service

Applying the proposed 2.5 per cent accrual rate to all years of service is a more satisfactory solution, except for members who will be leaving the House in the next six years, when their six-year average would consist of a mixture of the 'old' and 'new' sessional indemnity. In this case the notional sessional indemnity for years before 1998 should be considered to be $106,000, not $64,400.

If all members switch to the new plan on this basis, a question arises about the appropriate limit on years of service, as it is recommended that the required years of service be raised from 19 (to produce a maximum of 75 per cent of the old sessional indemnity) to 28 (to produce 70 per cent of the new indemnity).

Again, several options are available.

Option A: No further accrual for members who now have 19 years' service

This produces an anomaly between members with 19 years and those still accruing a benefit at present.

Option B: Limit all members elected before the 36th parliament to 19 years' service

This eliminates the first anomaly but introduces another one between current members and those elected to the 36th and subsequent parliaments.

Option C: Allow all members of the defined benefit plan to continue to accrue pensions up to 28 years' service

This would appear to be the most equitable solution, recognizing that the grossed-up sessional indemnity is more reflective of MPs' pre-tax disposable income, as compared to the current sessional indemnity. It is therefore reasonable to allow long-service members to accrue a pension of 70 per cent of the grossed-up sessional indemnity.

It should also be noted that members would be required to recommence contributions at 5.5 per cent of the grossed-up sessional indemnity.

In addition, there would be no sudden increase in accrued pension for those who ceased accruing some time ago. The pension would increase gradually until a total of 28 years' contributory service had been reached.

We would therefore recommend that, in regard to transitional measures for current members who remain in the defined benefit plan,

* the 2.5 per cent accrual rate be applied to all years of service, subject to a 28-year limit;
* for members leaving the House during the next six years, the six-year average salary be based on the grossed-up salary for 1998 and subsequent years and a notional grossed-up salary of $106,000 for 1997 and previous years;
* members who have ceased accruing benefits recommence accruing benefits and contribute at 5.5 per cent of grossed-up salary until a total of 28 years' contributory service has been reached; and
* a comparable grossing up of sessional indemnity (but not the extension of the accrual period) be applied to members of the Senate retiring in the next six years.